C-746   CAREER EXAMINATION SERIES

This is your
PASSBOOK for...

Social Worker

Test Preparation Study Guide
Questions & Answers

COPYRIGHT NOTICE

This book is SOLELY intended for, is sold ONLY to, and its use is RESTRICTED to individual, bona fide applicants or candidates who qualify by virtue of having seriously filed applications for appropriate license, certificate, professional and/or promotional advancement, higher school matriculation, scholarship, or other legitimate requirements of education and/or governmental authorities.

This book is NOT intended for use, class instruction, tutoring, training, duplication, copying, reprinting, excerption, or adaptation, etc., by:

1) Other publishers
2) Proprietors and/or Instructors of "Coaching" and/or Preparatory Courses
3) Personnel and/or Training Divisions of commercial, industrial, and governmental organizations
4) Schools, colleges, or universities and/or their departments and staffs, including teachers and other personnel
5) Testing Agencies or Bureaus
6) Study groups which seek by the purchase of a single volume to copy and/or duplicate and/or adapt this material for use by the group as a whole without having purchased individual volumes for each of the members of the group
7) Et al.

Such persons would be in violation of appropriate Federal and State statutes.

PROVISION OF LICENSING AGREEMENTS – Recognized educational, commercial, industrial, and governmental institutions and organizations, and others legitimately engaged in educational pursuits, including training, testing, and measurement activities, may address request for a licensing agreement to the copyright owners, who will determine whether, and under what conditions, including fees and charges, the materials in this book may be used them. In other words, a licensing facility exists for the legitimate use of the material in this book on other than an individual basis. However, it is asseverated and affirmed here that the material in this book CANNOT be used without the receipt of the express permission of such a licensing agreement from the Publishers. Inquiries re licensing should be addressed to the company, attention rights and permissions department.

All rights reserved, including the right of reproduction in whole or in part, in any form or by any means, electronic or mechanical, including photocopying, recording, or by any information storage and retrieval system, without permission in writing from the Publisher.

Copyright © 2024 by
National Learning Corporation

212 Michael Drive, Syosset, NY 11791
(516) 921-8888 • www.passbooks.com
E-mail: info@passbooks.com

PUBLISHED IN THE UNITED STATES OF AMERICA

PASSBOOK® SERIES

THE *PASSBOOK® SERIES* has been created to prepare applicants and candidates for the ultimate academic battlefield – the examination room.

At some time in our lives, each and every one of us may be required to take an examination – for validation, matriculation, admission, qualification, registration, certification, or licensure.

Based on the assumption that every applicant or candidate has met the basic formal educational standards, has taken the required number of courses, and read the necessary texts, the *PASSBOOK® SERIES* furnishes the one special preparation which may assure passing with confidence, instead of failing with insecurity. Examination questions – together with answers – are furnished as the basic vehicle for study so that the mysteries of the examination and its compounding difficulties may be eliminated or diminished by a sure method.

This book is meant to help you pass your examination provided that you qualify and are serious in your objective.

The entire field is reviewed through the huge store of content information which is succinctly presented through a provocative and challenging approach – the question-and-answer method.

A climate of success is established by furnishing the correct answers at the end of each test.

You soon learn to recognize types of questions, forms of questions, and patterns of questioning. You may even begin to anticipate expected outcomes.

You perceive that many questions are repeated or adapted so that you can gain acute insights, which may enable you to score many sure points.

You learn how to confront new questions, or types of questions, and to attack them confidently and work out the correct answers.

You note objectives and emphases, and recognize pitfalls and dangers, so that you may make positive educational adjustments.

Moreover, you are kept fully informed in relation to new concepts, methods, practices, and directions in the field.

You discover that you are actually taking the examination all the time: you are preparing for the examination by "taking" an examination, not by reading extraneous and/or supererogatory textbooks.

In short, this PASSBOOK®, used directedly, should be an important factor in helping you to pass your test.

SOCIAL WORKER

DUTIES

As a Social Worker, under direct supervision, you would perform a wide variety of social services depending upon the facility which you join and the specific unit and/or department in which you work. For example, you may be working in an inpatient or outpatient setting, or in a social services or community services department.

In whichever setting you work, your tasks would be likely to include a casework load, therapy work (individual and/or group), and work with community resources and services. Also, you would most likely be working as a member of an intra- or inter-disciplinary team, helping to make referrals and helping to organize and participate in various inter-disciplinary activities as part of a team.

EXAMPLES OF WORK

- Assesses child, family and community relationships of clients
- Develops social work treatment plans based on assessment of social needs
- Makes recommendations regarding appropriate placements or alternatives to placement for children at risk
- Functions as agency liaison with Probation Department, Family Court, County Attorney and placement agencies
- Refers children and families to community agencies
- Performs diagnostic assessments of children identified as at risk of placement, utilizing appropriate DSM-III R categories
- Provides consultation to agency staff regarding client service needs
- Provides in-service training to agency staff
- Provides therapeutic counseling to individuals and families experiencing severe dysfunctions
- Provides expert testimony in Family Court proceedings, including rendering opinions based on professional social work training and experience
- Organizes and leads group therapy sessions for children and adults on issues related to child welfare
- Keeps records of services being provided to serve in evaluations and planning of agency programs
- Participates in placement committee meetings and agency case conferences
- Provides agency administrators with information regarding current developments in the field of professional social work
- Prepares a variety of records and reports related to the work

SCOPE OF THE EXAMINATION

The <u>written test</u> will cover knowledge, skills and/or abilities in such areas as:

1. Case Histories in Social Services Casework Programs;
2. Principles and Practices of Social Casework;
3. Interviewing; and
4. Preparing Written Material.

HOW TO TAKE A TEST

I. YOU MUST PASS AN EXAMINATION

A. WHAT EVERY CANDIDATE SHOULD KNOW

Examination applicants often ask us for help in preparing for the written test. What can I study in advance? What kinds of questions will be asked? How will the test be given? How will the papers be graded?

As an applicant for a civil service examination, you may be wondering about some of these things. Our purpose here is to suggest effective methods of advance study and to describe civil service examinations.

Your chances for success on this examination can be increased if you know how to prepare. Those "pre-examination jitters" can be reduced if you know what to expect. You can even experience an adventure in good citizenship if you know why civil service exams are given.

B. WHY ARE CIVIL SERVICE EXAMINATIONS GIVEN?

Civil service examinations are important to you in two ways. As a citizen, you want public jobs filled by employees who know how to do their work. As a job seeker, you want a fair chance to compete for that job on an equal footing with other candidates. The best-known means of accomplishing this two-fold goal is the competitive examination.

Exams are widely publicized throughout the nation. They may be administered for jobs in federal, state, city, municipal, town or village governments or agencies.

Any citizen may apply, with some limitations, such as the age or residence of applicants. Your experience and education may be reviewed to see whether you meet the requirements for the particular examination. When these requirements exist, they are reasonable and applied consistently to all applicants. Thus, a competitive examination may cause you some uneasiness now, but it is your privilege and safeguard.

C. HOW ARE CIVIL SERVICE EXAMS DEVELOPED?

Examinations are carefully written by trained technicians who are specialists in the field known as "psychological measurement," in consultation with recognized authorities in the field of work that the test will cover. These experts recommend the subject matter areas or skills to be tested; only those knowledges or skills important to your success on the job are included. The most reliable books and source materials available are used as references. Together, the experts and technicians judge the difficulty level of the questions.

Test technicians know how to phrase questions so that the problem is clearly stated. Their ethics do not permit "trick" or "catch" questions. Questions may have been tried out on sample groups, or subjected to statistical analysis, to determine their usefulness.

Written tests are often used in combination with performance tests, ratings of training and experience, and oral interviews. All of these measures combine to form the best-known means of finding the right person for the right job.

II. HOW TO PASS THE WRITTEN TEST

A. NATURE OF THE EXAMINATION

To prepare intelligently for civil service examinations, you should know how they differ from school examinations you have taken. In school you were assigned certain definite pages to read or subjects to cover. The examination questions were quite detailed and usually emphasized memory. Civil service exams, on the other hand, try to discover your present ability to perform the duties of a position, plus your potentiality to learn these duties. In other words, a civil service exam attempts to predict how successful you will be. Questions cover such a broad area that they cannot be as minute and detailed as school exam questions.

In the public service similar kinds of work, or positions, are grouped together in one "class." This process is known as *position-classification*. All the positions in a class are paid according to the salary range for that class. One class title covers all of these positions, and they are all tested by the same examination.

B. FOUR BASIC STEPS

1) Study the announcement

How, then, can you know what subjects to study? Our best answer is: "Learn as much as possible about the class of positions for which you've applied." The exam will test the knowledge, skills and abilities needed to do the work.

Your most valuable source of information about the position you want is the official exam announcement. This announcement lists the training and experience qualifications. Check these standards and apply only if you come reasonably close to meeting them.

The brief description of the position in the examination announcement offers some clues to the subjects which will be tested. Think about the job itself. Review the duties in your mind. Can you perform them, or are there some in which you are rusty? Fill in the blank spots in your preparation.

Many jurisdictions preview the written test in the exam announcement by including a section called "Knowledge and Abilities Required," "Scope of the Examination," or some similar heading. Here you will find out specifically what fields will be tested.

2) Review your own background

Once you learn in general what the position is all about, and what you need to know to do the work, ask yourself which subjects you already know fairly well and which need improvement. You may wonder whether to concentrate on improving your strong areas or on building some background in your fields of weakness. When the announcement has specified "some knowledge" or "considerable knowledge," or has used adjectives like "beginning principles of..." or "advanced ... methods," you can get a clue as to the number and difficulty of questions to be asked in any given field. More questions, and hence broader coverage, would be included for those subjects which are more important in the work. Now weigh your strengths and weaknesses against the job requirements and prepare accordingly.

3) Determine the level of the position

Another way to tell how intensively you should prepare is to understand the level of the job for which you are applying. Is it the entering level? In other words, is this the position in which beginners in a field of work are hired? Or is it an intermediate or advanced level? Sometimes this is indicated by such words as "Junior" or "Senior" in the class title. Other jurisdictions use Roman numerals to designate the level – Clerk I, Clerk II, for example. The word "Supervisor" sometimes appears in the title. If the level is not indicated by the title, check the description of duties. Will you be working under very close supervision, or will you have responsibility for independent decisions in this work?

4) Choose appropriate study materials

Now that you know the subjects to be examined and the relative amount of each subject to be covered, you can choose suitable study materials. For beginning level jobs, or even advanced ones, if you have a pronounced weakness in some aspect of your training, read a modern, standard textbook in that field. Be sure it is up to date and has general coverage. Such books are normally available at your library, and the librarian will be glad to help you locate one. For entry-level positions, questions of appropriate difficulty are chosen – neither highly advanced questions, nor those too simple. Such questions require careful thought but not advanced training.

If the position for which you are applying is technical or advanced, you will read more advanced, specialized material. If you are already familiar with the basic principles of your field, elementary textbooks would waste your time. Concentrate on advanced textbooks and technical periodicals. Think through the concepts and review difficult problems in your field.

These are all general sources. You can get more ideas on your own initiative, following these leads. For example, training manuals and publications of the government agency which employs workers in your field can be useful, particularly for technical and professional positions. A letter or visit to the government department involved may result in more specific study suggestions, and certainly will provide you with a more definite idea of the exact nature of the position you are seeking.

III. KINDS OF TESTS

Tests are used for purposes other than measuring knowledge and ability to perform specified duties. For some positions, it is equally important to test ability to make adjustments to new situations or to profit from training. In others, basic mental abilities not dependent on information are essential. Questions which test these things may not appear as pertinent to the duties of the position as those which test for knowledge and information. Yet they are often highly important parts of a fair examination. For very general questions, it is almost impossible to help you direct your study efforts. What we can do is to point out some of the more common of these general abilities needed in public service positions and describe some typical questions.

1) General information

Broad, general information has been found useful for predicting job success in some kinds of work. This is tested in a variety of ways, from vocabulary lists to questions about current events. Basic background in some field of work, such as sociology or economics, may be sampled in a group of questions. Often these are principles which have become familiar to most persons through exposure rather than through formal training. It is difficult to advise you how to study for these questions; being alert to the world around you is our best suggestion.

2) Verbal ability

An example of an ability needed in many positions is verbal or language ability. Verbal ability is, in brief, the ability to use and understand words. Vocabulary and grammar tests are typical measures of this ability. Reading comprehension or paragraph interpretation questions are common in many kinds of civil service tests. You are given a paragraph of written material and asked to find its central meaning.

3) Numerical ability

Number skills can be tested by the familiar arithmetic problem, by checking paired lists of numbers to see which are alike and which are different, or by interpreting charts and graphs. In the latter test, a graph may be printed in the test booklet which you are asked to use as the basis for answering questions.

4) Observation

A popular test for law-enforcement positions is the observation test. A picture is shown to you for several minutes, then taken away. Questions about the picture test your ability to observe both details and larger elements.

5) Following directions

In many positions in the public service, the employee must be able to carry out written instructions dependably and accurately. You may be given a chart with several columns, each column listing a variety of information. The questions require you to carry out directions involving the information given in the chart.

6) Skills and aptitudes

Performance tests effectively measure some manual skills and aptitudes. When the skill is one in which you are trained, such as typing or shorthand, you can practice. These tests are often very much like those given in business school or high school courses. For many of the other skills and aptitudes, however, no short-time preparation can be made. Skills and abilities natural to you or that you have developed throughout your lifetime are being tested.

Many of the general questions just described provide all the data needed to answer the questions and ask you to use your reasoning ability to find the answers. Your best preparation for these tests, as well as for tests of facts and ideas, is to be at your physical and mental best. You, no doubt, have your own methods of getting into an exam-taking mood and keeping "in shape." The next section lists some ideas on this subject.

IV. KINDS OF QUESTIONS

Only rarely is the "essay" question, which you answer in narrative form, used in civil service tests. Civil service tests are usually of the short-answer type. Full instructions for answering these questions will be given to you at the examination. But in case this is your first experience with short-answer questions and separate answer sheets, here is what you need to know:

1) Multiple-choice Questions

Most popular of the short-answer questions is the "multiple choice" or "best answer" question. It can be used, for example, to test for factual knowledge, ability to solve problems or judgment in meeting situations found at work.

A multiple-choice question is normally one of three types—
- It can begin with an incomplete statement followed by several possible endings. You are to find the one ending which *best* completes the statement, although some of the others may not be entirely wrong.
- It can also be a complete statement in the form of a question which is answered by choosing one of the statements listed.

- It can be in the form of a problem – again you select the best answer.

Here is an example of a multiple-choice question with a discussion which should give you some clues as to the method for choosing the right answer:

When an employee has a complaint about his assignment, the action which will *best* help him overcome his difficulty is to
- A. discuss his difficulty with his coworkers
- B. take the problem to the head of the organization
- C. take the problem to the person who gave him the assignment
- D. say nothing to anyone about his complaint

In answering this question, you should study each of the choices to find which is best. Consider choice "A" – Certainly an employee may discuss his complaint with fellow employees, but no change or improvement can result, and the complaint remains unresolved. Choice "B" is a poor choice since the head of the organization probably does not know what assignment you have been given, and taking your problem to him is known as "going over the head" of the supervisor. The supervisor, or person who made the assignment, is the person who can clarify it or correct any injustice. Choice "C" is, therefore, correct. To say nothing, as in choice "D," is unwise. Supervisors have and interest in knowing the problems employees are facing, and the employee is seeking a solution to his problem.

2) True/False Questions

The "true/false" or "right/wrong" form of question is sometimes used. Here a complete statement is given. Your job is to decide whether the statement is right or wrong.

SAMPLE: A roaming cell-phone call to a nearby city costs less than a non-roaming call to a distant city.

This statement is wrong, or false, since roaming calls are more expensive.

This is not a complete list of all possible question forms, although most of the others are variations of these common types. You will always get complete directions for answering questions. Be sure you understand *how* to mark your answers – ask questions until you do.

V. RECORDING YOUR ANSWERS

Computer terminals are used more and more today for many different kinds of exams.
For an examination with very few applicants, you may be told to record your answers in the test booklet itself. Separate answer sheets are much more common. If this separate answer sheet is to be scored by machine – and this is often the case – it is highly important that you mark your answers correctly in order to get credit.
An electronic scoring machine is often used in civil service offices because of the speed with which papers can be scored. Machine-scored answer sheets must be marked with a pencil, which will be given to you. This pencil has a high graphite content which responds to the electronic scoring machine. As a matter of fact, stray dots may register as answers, so do not let your pencil rest on the answer sheet while you are pondering the correct answer. Also, if your pencil lead breaks or is otherwise defective, ask for another.

Since the answer sheet will be dropped in a slot in the scoring machine, be careful not to bend the corners or get the paper crumpled.

The answer sheet normally has five vertical columns of numbers, with 30 numbers to a column. These numbers correspond to the question numbers in your test booklet. After each number, going across the page are four or five pairs of dotted lines. These short dotted lines have small letters or numbers above them. The first two pairs may also have a "T" or "F" above the letters. This indicates that the first two pairs only are to be used if the questions are of the true-false type. If the questions are multiple choice, disregard the "T" and "F" and pay attention only to the small letters or numbers.

Answer your questions in the manner of the sample that follows:

32. The largest city in the United States is
    A. Washington, D.C.
    B. New York City
    C. Chicago
    D. Detroit
    E. San Francisco

1) Choose the answer you think is best. (New York City is the largest, so "B" is correct.)
2) Find the row of dotted lines numbered the same as the question you are answering. (Find row number 32)
3) Find the pair of dotted lines corresponding to the answer. (Find the pair of lines under the mark "B.")
4) Make a solid black mark between the dotted lines.

VI. BEFORE THE TEST

Common sense will help you find procedures to follow to get ready for an examination. Too many of us, however, overlook these sensible measures. Indeed, nervousness and fatigue have been found to be the most serious reasons why applicants fail to do their best on civil service tests. Here is a list of reminders:

- Begin your preparation early – Don't wait until the last minute to go scurrying around for books and materials or to find out what the position is all about.
- Prepare continuously – An hour a night for a week is better than an all-night cram session. This has been definitely established. What is more, a night a week for a month will return better dividends than crowding your study into a shorter period of time.
- Locate the place of the exam – You have been sent a notice telling you when and where to report for the examination. If the location is in a different town or otherwise unfamiliar to you, it would be well to inquire the best route and learn something about the building.
- Relax the night before the test – Allow your mind to rest. Do not study at all that night. Plan some mild recreation or diversion; then go to bed early and get a good night's sleep.
- Get up early enough to make a leisurely trip to the place for the test – This way unforeseen events, traffic snarls, unfamiliar buildings, etc. will not upset you.
- Dress comfortably – A written test is not a fashion show. You will be known by number and not by name, so wear something comfortable.

- Leave excess paraphernalia at home – Shopping bags and odd bundles will get in your way. You need bring only the items mentioned in the official notice you received; usually everything you need is provided. Do not bring reference books to the exam. They will only confuse those last minutes and be taken away from you when in the test room.
- Arrive somewhat ahead of time – If because of transportation schedules you must get there very early, bring a newspaper or magazine to take your mind off yourself while waiting.
- Locate the examination room – When you have found the proper room, you will be directed to the seat or part of the room where you will sit. Sometimes you are given a sheet of instructions to read while you are waiting. Do not fill out any forms until you are told to do so; just read them and be prepared.
- Relax and prepare to listen to the instructions
- If you have any physical problem that may keep you from doing your best, be sure to tell the test administrator. If you are sick or in poor health, you really cannot do your best on the exam. You can come back and take the test some other time.

VII. AT THE TEST

The day of the test is here and you have the test booklet in your hand. The temptation to get going is very strong. Caution! There is more to success than knowing the right answers. You must know how to identify your papers and understand variations in the type of short-answer question used in this particular examination. Follow these suggestions for maximum results from your efforts:

1) Cooperate with the monitor

The test administrator has a duty to create a situation in which you can be as much at ease as possible. He will give instructions, tell you when to begin, check to see that you are marking your answer sheet correctly, and so on. He is not there to guard you, although he will see that your competitors do not take unfair advantage. He wants to help you do your best.

2) Listen to all instructions

Don't jump the gun! Wait until you understand all directions. In most civil service tests you get more time than you need to answer the questions. So don't be in a hurry. Read each word of instructions until you clearly understand the meaning. Study the examples, listen to all announcements and follow directions. Ask questions if you do not understand what to do.

3) Identify your papers

Civil service exams are usually identified by number only. You will be assigned a number; you must not put your name on your test papers. Be sure to copy your number correctly. Since more than one exam may be given, copy your exact examination title.

4) Plan your time

Unless you are told that a test is a "speed" or "rate of work" test, speed itself is usually not important. Time enough to answer all the questions will be provided, but this does not mean that you have all day. An overall time limit has been set. Divide the total time (in minutes) by the number of questions to determine the approximate time you have for each question.

5) Do not linger over difficult questions

If you come across a difficult question, mark it with a paper clip (useful to have along) and come back to it when you have been through the booklet. One caution if you do this – be sure to skip a number on your answer sheet as well. Check often to be sure that you have not lost your place and that you are marking in the row numbered the same as the question you are answering.

6) Read the questions

Be sure you know what the question asks! Many capable people are unsuccessful because they failed to *read* the questions correctly.

7) Answer all questions

Unless you have been instructed that a penalty will be deducted for incorrect answers, it is better to guess than to omit a question.

8) Speed tests

It is often better NOT to guess on speed tests. It has been found that on timed tests people are tempted to spend the last few seconds before time is called in marking answers at random – without even reading them – in the hope of picking up a few extra points. To discourage this practice, the instructions may warn you that your score will be "corrected" for guessing. That is, a penalty will be applied. The incorrect answers will be deducted from the correct ones, or some other penalty formula will be used.

9) Review your answers

If you finish before time is called, go back to the questions you guessed or omitted to give them further thought. Review other answers if you have time.

10) Return your test materials

If you are ready to leave before others have finished or time is called, take ALL your materials to the monitor and leave quietly. Never take any test material with you. The monitor can discover whose papers are not complete, and taking a test booklet may be grounds for disqualification.

VIII. EXAMINATION TECHNIQUES

1) Read the general instructions carefully. These are usually printed on the first page of the exam booklet. As a rule, these instructions refer to the timing of the examination; the fact that you should not start work until the signal and must stop work at a signal, etc. If there are any *special* instructions, such as a choice of questions to be answered, make sure that you note this instruction carefully.

2) When you are ready to start work on the examination, that is as soon as the signal has been given, read the instructions to each question booklet, underline any key words or phrases, such as *least, best, outline, describe* and the like. In this way you will tend to answer as requested rather than discover on reviewing your paper that you *listed without describing*, that you selected the *worst* choice rather than the *best* choice, etc.

3) If the examination is of the objective or multiple-choice type – that is, each question will also give a series of possible answers: A, B, C or D, and you are called upon to select the best answer and write the letter next to that answer on your answer paper – it is advisable to start answering each question in turn. There may be anywhere from 50 to 100 such questions in the three or four hours allotted and you can see how much time would be taken if you read through all the questions before beginning to answer any. Furthermore, if you come across a question or group of questions which you know would be difficult to answer, it would undoubtedly affect your handling of all the other questions.

4) If the examination is of the essay type and contains but a few questions, it is a moot point as to whether you should read all the questions before starting to answer any one. Of course, if you are given a choice – say five out of seven and the like – then it is essential to read all the questions so you can eliminate the two that are most difficult. If, however, you are asked to answer all the questions, there may be danger in trying to answer the easiest one first because you may find that you will spend too much time on it. The best technique is to answer the first question, then proceed to the second, etc.

5) Time your answers. Before the exam begins, write down the time it started, then add the time allowed for the examination and write down the time it must be completed, then divide the time available somewhat as follows:
   - If 3-1/2 hours are allowed, that would be 210 minutes. If you have 80 objective-type questions, that would be an average of 2-1/2 minutes per question. Allow yourself no more than 2 minutes per question, or a total of 160 minutes, which will permit about 50 minutes to review.
   - If for the time allotment of 210 minutes there are 7 essay questions to answer, that would average about 30 minutes a question. Give yourself only 25 minutes per question so that you have about 35 minutes to review.

6) The most important instruction is to *read each question* and make sure you know what is wanted. The second most important instruction is to *time yourself properly* so that you answer every question. The third most important instruction is to *answer every question*. Guess if you have to but include something for each question. Remember that you will receive no credit for a blank and will probably receive some credit if you write something in answer to an essay question. If you guess a letter – say "B" for a multiple-choice question – you may have guessed right. If you leave a blank as an answer to a multiple-choice question, the examiners may respect your feelings but it will not add a point to your score. Some exams may penalize you for wrong answers, so in such cases *only*, you may not want to guess unless you have some basis for your answer.

7) Suggestions
   a. Objective-type questions
      1. Examine the question booklet for proper sequence of pages and questions
      2. Read all instructions carefully
      3. Skip any question which seems too difficult; return to it after all other questions have been answered
      4. Apportion your time properly; do not spend too much time on any single question or group of questions

5. Note and underline key words – *all, most, fewest, least, best, worst, same, opposite,* etc.
6. Pay particular attention to negatives
7. Note unusual option, e.g., unduly long, short, complex, different or similar in content to the body of the question
8. Observe the use of "hedging" words – *probably, may, most likely,* etc.
9. Make sure that your answer is put next to the same number as the question
10. Do not second-guess unless you have good reason to believe the second answer is definitely more correct
11. Cross out original answer if you decide another answer is more accurate; do not erase until you are ready to hand your paper in
12. Answer all questions; guess unless instructed otherwise
13. Leave time for review

   b. Essay questions
   1. Read each question carefully
   2. Determine exactly what is wanted. Underline key words or phrases.
   3. Decide on outline or paragraph answer
   4. Include many different points and elements unless asked to develop any one or two points or elements
   5. Show impartiality by giving pros and cons unless directed to select one side only
   6. Make and write down any assumptions you find necessary to answer the questions
   7. Watch your English, grammar, punctuation and choice of words
   8. Time your answers; don't crowd material

8) Answering the essay question

Most essay questions can be answered by framing the specific response around several key words or ideas. Here are a few such key words or ideas:

M's: manpower, materials, methods, money, management
P's: purpose, program, policy, plan, procedure, practice, problems, pitfalls, personnel, public relations
   a. Six basic steps in handling problems:
   1. Preliminary plan and background development
   2. Collect information, data and facts
   3. Analyze and interpret information, data and facts
   4. Analyze and develop solutions as well as make recommendations
   5. Prepare report and sell recommendations
   6. Install recommendations and follow up effectiveness

   b. Pitfalls to avoid
   1. *Taking things for granted* – A statement of the situation does not necessarily imply that each of the elements is necessarily true; for example, a complaint may be invalid and biased so that all that can be taken for granted is that a complaint has been registered

2. *Considering only one side of a situation* – Wherever possible, indicate several alternatives and then point out the reasons you selected the best one
3. *Failing to indicate follow up* – Whenever your answer indicates action on your part, make certain that you will take proper follow-up action to see how successful your recommendations, procedures or actions turn out to be
4. *Taking too long in answering any single question* – Remember to time your answers properly

IX. AFTER THE TEST

Scoring procedures differ in detail among civil service jurisdictions although the general principles are the same. Whether the papers are hand-scored or graded by machine we have described, they are nearly always graded by number. That is, the person who marks the paper knows only the number – never the name – of the applicant. Not until all the papers have been graded will they be matched with names. If other tests, such as training and experience or oral interview ratings have been given, scores will be combined. Different parts of the examination usually have different weights. For example, the written test might count 60 percent of the final grade, and a rating of training and experience 40 percent. In many jurisdictions, veterans will have a certain number of points added to their grades.

After the final grade has been determined, the names are placed in grade order and an eligible list is established. There are various methods for resolving ties between those who get the same final grade – probably the most common is to place first the name of the person whose application was received first. Job offers are made from the eligible list in the order the names appear on it. You will be notified of your grade and your rank as soon as all these computations have been made. This will be done as rapidly as possible.

People who are found to meet the requirements in the announcement are called "eligibles." Their names are put on a list of eligible candidates. An eligible's chances of getting a job depend on how high he stands on this list and how fast agencies are filling jobs from the list.

When a job is to be filled from a list of eligibles, the agency asks for the names of people on the list of eligibles for that job. When the civil service commission receives this request, it sends to the agency the names of the three people highest on this list. Or, if the job to be filled has specialized requirements, the office sends the agency the names of the top three persons who meet these requirements from the general list.

The appointing officer makes a choice from among the three people whose names were sent to him. If the selected person accepts the appointment, the names of the others are put back on the list to be considered for future openings.

That is the rule in hiring from all kinds of eligible lists, whether they are for typist, carpenter, chemist, or something else. For every vacancy, the appointing officer has his choice of any one of the top three eligibles on the list. This explains why the person whose name is on top of the list sometimes does not get an appointment when some of the persons lower on the list do. If the appointing officer chooses the second or third eligible, the No. 1 eligible does not get a job at once, but stays on the list until he is appointed or the list is terminated.

X. HOW TO PASS THE INTERVIEW TEST

The examination for which you applied requires an oral interview test. You have already taken the written test and you are now being called for the interview test – the final part of the formal examination.

You may think that it is not possible to prepare for an interview test and that there are no procedures to follow during an interview. Our purpose is to point out some things you can do in advance that will help you and some good rules to follow and pitfalls to avoid while you are being interviewed.

What is an interview supposed to test?

The written examination is designed to test the technical knowledge and competence of the candidate; the oral is designed to evaluate intangible qualities, not readily measured otherwise, and to establish a list showing the relative fitness of each candidate – as measured against his competitors – for the position sought. Scoring is not on the basis of "right" and "wrong," but on a sliding scale of values ranging from "not passable" to "outstanding." As a matter of fact, it is possible to achieve a relatively low score without a single "incorrect" answer because of evident weakness in the qualities being measured.

Occasionally, an examination may consist entirely of an oral test – either an individual or a group oral. In such cases, information is sought concerning the technical knowledges and abilities of the candidate, since there has been no written examination for this purpose. More commonly, however, an oral test is used to supplement a written examination.

Who conducts interviews?

The composition of oral boards varies among different jurisdictions. In nearly all, a representative of the personnel department serves as chairman. One of the members of the board may be a representative of the department in which the candidate would work. In some cases, "outside experts" are used, and, frequently, a businessman or some other representative of the general public is asked to serve. Labor and management or other special groups may be represented. The aim is to secure the services of experts in the appropriate field.

However the board is composed, it is a good idea (and not at all improper or unethical) to ascertain in advance of the interview who the members are and what groups they represent. When you are introduced to them, you will have some idea of their backgrounds and interests, and at least you will not stutter and stammer over their names.

What should be done before the interview?

While knowledge about the board members is useful and takes some of the surprise element out of the interview, there is other preparation which is more substantive. It *is* possible to prepare for an oral interview – in several ways:

1) Keep a copy of your application and review it carefully before the interview

This may be the only document before the oral board, and the starting point of the interview. Know what education and experience you have listed there, and the sequence and dates of all of it. Sometimes the board will ask you to review the highlights of your experience for them; you should not have to hem and haw doing it.

2) Study the class specification and the examination announcement

Usually, the oral board has one or both of these to guide them. The qualities, characteristics or knowledges required by the position sought are stated in these documents. They offer valuable clues as to the nature of the oral interview. For example, if the job involves supervisory responsibilities, the announcement will usually indicate that knowledge of modern supervisory methods and the qualifications of the candidate as a supervisor will be tested. If so, you can expect such questions, frequently in the form of a hypothetical situation which you are expected to solve. NEVER go into an oral without knowledge of the duties and responsibilities of the job you seek.

3) Think through each qualification required

Try to visualize the kind of questions you would ask if you were a board member. How well could you answer them? Try especially to appraise your own knowledge and background in each area, *measured against the job sought*, and identify any areas in which you are weak. Be critical and realistic – do not flatter yourself.

4) Do some general reading in areas in which you feel you may be weak

For example, if the job involves supervision and your past experience has NOT, some general reading in supervisory methods and practices, particularly in the field of human relations, might be useful. Do NOT study agency procedures or detailed manuals. The oral board will be testing your understanding and capacity, not your memory.

5) Get a good night's sleep and watch your general health and mental attitude

You will want a clear head at the interview. Take care of a cold or any other minor ailment, and of course, no hangovers.

What should be done on the day of the interview?

Now comes the day of the interview itself. Give yourself plenty of time to get there. Plan to arrive somewhat ahead of the scheduled time, particularly if your appointment is in the fore part of the day. If a previous candidate fails to appear, the board might be ready for you a bit early. By early afternoon an oral board is almost invariably behind schedule if there are many candidates, and you may have to wait. Take along a book or magazine to read, or your application to review, but leave any extraneous material in the waiting room when you go in for your interview. In any event, relax and compose yourself.

The matter of dress is important. The board is forming impressions about you – from your experience, your manners, your attitude, and your appearance. Give your personal appearance careful attention. Dress your best, but not your flashiest. Choose conservative, appropriate clothing, and be sure it is immaculate. This is a business interview, and your appearance should indicate that you regard it as such. Besides, being well groomed and properly dressed will help boost your confidence.

Sooner or later, someone will call your name and escort you into the interview room. *This is it.* From here on you are on your own. It is too late for any more preparation. But remember, you asked for this opportunity to prove your fitness, and you are here because your request was granted.

What happens when you go in?

The usual sequence of events will be as follows: The clerk (who is often the board stenographer) will introduce you to the chairman of the oral board, who will introduce you to the other members of the board. Acknowledge the introductions before you sit down. Do not be surprised if you find a microphone facing you or a stenotypist sitting by. Oral interviews are usually recorded in the event of an appeal or other review.

Usually the chairman of the board will open the interview by reviewing the highlights of your education and work experience from your application – primarily for the benefit of the other members of the board, as well as to get the material into the record. Do not interrupt or comment unless there is an error or significant misinterpretation; if that is the case, do not hesitate. But do not quibble about insignificant matters. Also, he will usually ask you some question about your education, experience or your present job – partly to get you to start talking and to establish the interviewing "rapport." He may start the actual questioning, or turn it over to one of the other members. Frequently, each member undertakes the questioning on a particular area, one in which he is perhaps most competent, so you can expect each member to participate in the examination. Because time is limited, you may also expect some rather abrupt switches in the direction the questioning takes, so do not be upset by it. Normally, a board member will not pursue a single line of questioning unless he discovers a particular strength or weakness.

After each member has participated, the chairman will usually ask whether any member has any further questions, then will ask you if you have anything you wish to add. Unless you are expecting this question, it may floor you. Worse, it may start you off on an extended, extemporaneous speech. The board is not usually seeking more information. The question is principally to offer you a last opportunity to present further qualifications or to indicate that you have nothing to add. So, if you feel that a significant qualification or characteristic has been overlooked, it is proper to point it out in a sentence or so. Do not compliment the board on the thoroughness of their examination – they have been sketchy, and you know it. If you wish, merely say, "No thank you, I have nothing further to add." This is a point where you can "talk yourself out" of a good impression or fail to present an important bit of information. Remember, *you close the interview yourself*.

The chairman will then say, "That is all, Mr. _____, thank you." Do not be startled; the interview is over, and quicker than you think. Thank him, gather your belongings and take your leave. Save your sigh of relief for the other side of the door.

How to put your best foot forward

Throughout this entire process, you may feel that the board individually and collectively is trying to pierce your defenses, seek out your hidden weaknesses and embarrass and confuse you. Actually, this is not true. They are obliged to make an appraisal of your qualifications for the job you are seeking, and they want to see you in your best light. Remember, they must interview all candidates and a non-cooperative candidate may become a failure in spite of their best efforts to bring out his qualifications. Here are 15 suggestions that will help you:

1) Be natural – Keep your attitude confident, not cocky

If you are not confident that you can do the job, do not expect the board to be. Do not apologize for your weaknesses, try to bring out your strong points. The board is interested in a positive, not negative, presentation. Cockiness will antagonize any board member and make him wonder if you are covering up a weakness by a false show of strength.

2) Get comfortable, but don't lounge or sprawl

Sit erectly but not stiffly. A careless posture may lead the board to conclude that you are careless in other things, or at least that you are not impressed by the importance of the occasion. Either conclusion is natural, even if incorrect. Do not fuss with your clothing, a pencil or an ashtray. Your hands may occasionally be useful to emphasize a point; do not let them become a point of distraction.

3) Do not wisecrack or make small talk

This is a serious situation, and your attitude should show that you consider it as such. Further, the time of the board is limited – they do not want to waste it, and neither should you.

4) Do not exaggerate your experience or abilities
In the first place, from information in the application or other interviews and sources, the board may know more about you than you think. Secondly, you probably will not get away with it. An experienced board is rather adept at spotting such a situation, so do not take the chance.

5) If you know a board member, do not make a point of it, yet do not hide it
Certainly you are not fooling him, and probably not the other members of the board. Do not try to take advantage of your acquaintanceship – it will probably do you little good.

6) Do not dominate the interview
Let the board do that. They will give you the clues – do not assume that you have to do all the talking. Realize that the board has a number of questions to ask you, and do not try to take up all the interview time by showing off your extensive knowledge of the answer to the first one.

7) Be attentive
You only have 20 minutes or so, and you should keep your attention at its sharpest throughout. When a member is addressing a problem or question to you, give him your undivided attention. Address your reply principally to him, but do not exclude the other board members.

8) Do not interrupt
A board member may be stating a problem for you to analyze. He will ask you a question when the time comes. Let him state the problem, and wait for the question.

9) Make sure you understand the question
Do not try to answer until you are sure what the question is. If it is not clear, restate it in your own words or ask the board member to clarify it for you. However, do not haggle about minor elements.

10) Reply promptly but not hastily
A common entry on oral board rating sheets is "candidate responded readily," or "candidate hesitated in replies." Respond as promptly and quickly as you can, but do not jump to a hasty, ill-considered answer.

11) Do not be peremptory in your answers
A brief answer is proper – but do not fire your answer back. That is a losing game from your point of view. The board member can probably ask questions much faster than you can answer them.

12) Do not try to create the answer you think the board member wants
He is interested in what kind of mind you have and how it works – not in playing games. Furthermore, he can usually spot this practice and will actually grade you down on it.

13) Do not switch sides in your reply merely to agree with a board member
Frequently, a member will take a contrary position merely to draw you out and to see if you are willing and able to defend your point of view. Do not start a debate, yet do not surrender a good position. If a position is worth taking, it is worth defending.

14) Do not be afraid to admit an error in judgment if you are shown to be wrong
The board knows that you are forced to reply without any opportunity for careful consideration. Your answer may be demonstrably wrong. If so, admit it and get on with the interview.

15) Do not dwell at length on your present job
The opening question may relate to your present assignment. Answer the question but do not go into an extended discussion. You are being examined for a *new* job, not your present one. As a matter of fact, try to phrase ALL your answers in terms of the job for which you are being examined.

Basis of Rating
Probably you will forget most of these "do's" and "don'ts" when you walk into the oral interview room. Even remembering them all will not ensure you a passing grade. Perhaps you did not have the qualifications in the first place. But remembering them will help you to put your best foot forward, without treading on the toes of the board members.

Rumor and popular opinion to the contrary notwithstanding, an oral board wants you to make the best appearance possible. They know you are under pressure – but they also want to see how you respond to it as a guide to what your reaction would be under the pressures of the job you seek. They will be influenced by the degree of poise you display, the personal traits you show and the manner in which you respond.

ABOUT THIS BOOK

This book contains tests divided into Examination Sections. Go through each test, answering every question in the margin. We have also attached a sample answer sheet at the back of the book that can be removed and used. At the end of each test look at the answer key and check your answers. On the ones you got wrong, look at the right answer choice and learn. Do not fill in the answers first. Do not memorize the questions and answers, but understand the answer and principles involved. On your test, the questions will likely be different from the samples. Questions are changed and new ones added. If you understand these past questions you should have success with any changes that arise. Tests may consist of several types of questions. We have additional books on each subject should more study be advisable or necessary for you. Finally, the more you study, the better prepared you will be. This book is intended to be the last thing you study before you walk into the examination room. Prior study of relevant texts is also recommended. NLC publishes some of these in our Fundamental Series. Knowledge and good sense are important factors in passing your exam. Good luck also helps. So now study this Passbook, absorb the material contained within and take that knowledge into the examination. Then do your best to pass that exam.

EXAMINATION SECTION

EXAMINATION SECTION
TEST 1

DIRECTIONS: Each question or incomplete statement is followed by several suggested answers or completions. Select the one the BEST answers the question or completes the statement. *PRINT THE LETTER OF THE CORRECT ANSWER IN THE SPACE AT THE RIGHT.*

1. The primary sources of data in most assessments are

    A. completed assessment forms
    B. the client's verbal statements
    C. psychological test results
    D. collateral sources

2. A social worker is fulfilling the role of a "mediator" when he or she

    A. calls attention to the probable social consequences to a new housing development
    B. refers a jobless person to an unemployment agency
    C. evaluates the outcome of a colleague's practice
    D. helps a frustrated wife to clarify her position to a husband

3. In the systems model of human behavior, "division of labor" is an example of

    A. autopoiesis
    B. social control
    C. differentiation
    D. hierarchy

4. After several weeks of behavioral intervention, a child is consistently performing the desired behavior targeted by his parents and a social worker: that is, he is going to bed at the correct time without argument or delaying tactics. Now that he's reached this stage, the social worker recommends that the parents gradually withdraw the prompts and reinforcements that induced the behavior to begin with. This is an example of

    A. extinction
    B. shaping
    C. fading
    D. modeling

5. When working with a group, a social worker encourages decision-making by consensus. Drawbacks to the use of consensus include

    A. involvement of few available group resources
    B. alienation of the minority
    C. time- and energy-intensiveness
    D. decreased likelihood of handling future controversies

6. The primary rationale for the use of a social history for client assessment is that

    A. past behavior is the best predictor of future behavior
    B. the best source of information about a client's situation is the client her/himself
    C. the best protection against legal liability is an exhaustive data set

D. problems exist because of an unbalanced reaction between a client system and the environment

7. Most professional codes of ethics provide that a social worker's primary ethical duty is to

   A. respect client privacy and confidentiality
   B. challenge social injustice
   C. work in the best interest of clients
   D. avoid situations that involve ethical conflicts

8. In agency planning, which of the following visual aids will be MOST useful in helping to examine the benefits and drawbacks of different alternative choices

   A. Task planning sheet
   B. Gantt chart
   C. Decision tree
   D. PERT chart

9. Which of the following questions or statements is MOST appropriate for a practitioner in initiating an interview?

   A. "I understand you have a problem."
   B. "You came in here to see me about _____."
   C. "How can I help you today?"
   D. "I'm glad you came in to see me

10. What is the term commonly used to describe children who suffer physical, mental, or emotional injuries inflicted by caretaking adults?

    A. Developmentally disabled
    B. Victims
    C. At risk
    D. Abused or neglected

11. Typically, the questioning process in a social work interview should progress

    A. chronologically
    B. from general to specific
    C. from specific to general
    D. in a series of grouped topical units

12. Assessment is a process that is considered to be the task of the

    A. agency psychiatrist or clinician
    B. social worker
    C. client
    D. social worker and client together

13. A social worker who wants to use a small group as a resource for clients should remember the general rule that the addition of new members, especially resistant ones, should be avoided during the _____ stage of group development.

    A. differentiation
    B. intimacy

C. preaffiliation
D. power and control

14. During an assessment interview with a male high school student, it becomes clear to the practitioner that the boy's behavior problems are related in some way to his frustration at the different expectations of his teachers and his peers concerning the role of a student. The boy is experiencing

    A. inter-role conflict
    B. role ambiguity
    C. intra-role conflict
    D. role incapacity

15. When considering the use of informal resources for an intervention, the social worker should

    A. view informal resources as an inexpensive alternative to formal services
    B. whenever possible, try to "professionalize" or train informal resources to lend them authority
    C. already have some knowledge of available self-help groups in the community
    D. whenever informal resources are identified, try to steer clients toward the ones that are probably most useful

16. Probably the biggest difference between the supervisory role in social work and that of other professions is the

    A. amount of psychological support that must be provided to supervisees
    B. degree of direct involvement in the work of supervisees
    C. predominant use of "soft" criteria in performance evaluations
    D. greater difficulty in matching workers to tasks

17. A social worker is interviewing a woman in a mental hospital who appears lucid but is suspected of having some mental illness. When gathering information, the worker should

    A. explain fully the reason for the interview and ask the client to give her opinion of her mental status
    B. ask short, closed-ended assessment questions up front
    C. administer a standardized assessment that may be evaluated by a psychologist
    D. work assessment questions into the ordinary flow of the conversation

18. A social worker becomes aware of a colleague's incompetent or unethical practice. According to the NASW code, the worker's FIRST obligation is to

    A. inform all of the colleague's relevant clients of the situation
    B. approach the colleague to discuss his/her incapacitation, incompetence, etc.
    C. file a complaint with the NASW
    D. file a complaint with the appropriate licensing board

19. A "communication loop" is completed when

    A. the person to whom the message is addressed begins to respond
    B. the person who initiates the message has completed the transmission
    C. the person to whom the message is addressed receives the message
    D. the person to whom the message is addressed decodes the message

20. Because many parents believe in and utilize corporal punishment as discipline, a social worker must be able to differentiate physical abuse from ordinary spanking or corporal punishment. Which of the following is NOT a useful means of making this distinction?

    A. Parent striking the child in places that are easily injured
    B. Repeated episodes of corporal punishment
    C. Child's report that punishments are severe and painful
    D. Injury to child's body tissue

21. A social worker makes an initial in-home visit to a married couple who have willingly submitted to an intervention regarding their marital problems. During the interview the couple points out that they will be leaving the area in a few weeks, because the wife has been transferred by her employer to a new location. Probably the MOST appropriate plan for dealing with this couple would involve the _____ model of social work.

    A. person-centered
    B. cognitive-behavioral
    C. solution-focused
    D. task-centered

22. The primary purpose of evaluative research in social work is to

    A. measure a client's self-satisfaction
    B. determine whether outcomes can be attributed to an intervention
    C. express the effectiveness of interventions in material terms
    D. determine whether an outcome was achieved

23. Each of the following should be used as a guideline in child placement decisions, EXCEPT

    A. efforts to protect the child should involve as little disruption as possible
    B. use of placement to compel a parent to take some action
    C. involvement of parents and child in the placement decision
    D. maintenance of child's cultural beliefs in placement

24. Which of the following is NOT a factor involved in the decoding of a message?

    A. Relationship with interviewer
    B. Social, emotional, and cognitive barriers
    C. Ethics
    D. Context of interview

25. A practitioner wants to make the parents of an adolescent aware of the behavioral manifestations of depression. Which of the following is LEAST likely to be an indicator?

    A. Sudden tearful reactions
    B. Excessive pleasure-seeking
    C. Decline in school achievement
    D. Jokes about death or dying

26. Which of the following is LEAST likely to be an area of conflict between social workers and attorneys

A. Confidentiality
B. Recording information
C. The best interests of a client
D. The definition of "client"

27. Which of the following typically occurs in the first stage of group therapy?

    A. The members are hostile toward the leader.
    B. Cliques form within the group.
    C. The members talk through the leader and seem to ignore one another.
    D. The members interact with each other tend to ignore the leader.

28. In conducting employee evaluations, a social work supervisor should use _____ as available criteria.
    I.   pre-established objective measures such as timeliness
    II. "soft" criteria such as attitude
    III. the supervisor's own work experience
    IV. the performance of others in similar assignments

    A. I only
    B. I and II
    C. I and III
    D. I, II, III and IV

29. Which of the following is NOT a term that is interchangeable with "stepfamily"?

    A. Remarried family
    B. Blended family
    C. Reconstituted family
    D. Renested family

30. A worker refers a client to a colleague who specializes and is trained in law, even though the client requested the service from the worker. Which of the following professional values or ethics is the worker implementing?

    A. Self-determination
    B. Privacy
    C. Competence
    D. Confidentiality

31. Social work practice that is based on behavioral theory assumes that behaviors are determined by

    A. emotions
    B. consequences
    C. values
    D. internal thought processes

32. Which of the following is NOT a symptom associated with bipolar disorder?

    A. Increase in goal-oriented activity
    B. Distractibility
    C. Significant weight loss
    D. Decreased need for sleep

33. A 'helping relationship" between the social worker and client is BEST described as   33.____
    A. the goal of any initial contact between worker and client
    B. the medium offered to people in trouble through which they are presented with opportunities
    C. the means by which a worker gains the client's trust to solve problems
    D. a lifeline that is thrown to people in trouble in order to help them out of current problems

34. Communities often contain individuals who are categorized as "AFDC mothers" or "hard-core unemployed" or "AIDS patients," among others. This is a destructive application of the concept of   34.____

    A. service delivery
    B. niche
    C. differentiation
    D. diversity

35. The first step in any single-system practice evaluation is to   35.____

    A. record baseline data
    B. select suitable measures
    C. implement the intervention
    D. specify the goal

36. A social worker plans a behavioral intervention for a developmentally disabled adult who does not look people in the eye when speaking with them.   36.____
    Each of the following behavioral strategies may be useful to the intervention, EXCEPT

    A. overcorrection
    B. instruction
    C. prompting
    D. shaping

37. During several in-home visits with a family, the mother repeatedly refuses to acknowledge that her alcoholism is having an adverse effect on others in the household. The MOST appropriate next step for the social worker would be to initiate   37.____

    A. a challenge
    B. behavioral rehearsal
    C. self-talk management
    D. a behavioral contract

38. Working-class or low-income marriages are typically characterized by   38.____

    A. marriage late in life
    B. flexible divisions of labor
    C. troubled mother-child relationships
    D. emotional distance between partners

39. A researcher repeatedly measures the dependent variable throughout two baseline and two treatment phases of a study to assess whether variability in the dependent variable is due to the influence of the independent variable. She is using a(n) _____ design of measurement.   39.____

A. AB
B. ABAB
C. multiple baseline
D. Solomon four-group

40. What is the typical time-frame for crisis intervention? 40.____

    A. One to two weeks
    B. Six to eight weeks
    C. At least eight weeks
    D. Six months or more, depending on the nature of the crisis

41. Stigma, once it has become part of a culture, has certain predictable consequences. 41.____
    Which of the following is NOT one of these consequences?

    A. Discrimination
    B. Absorption
    C. Altered self-concept
    D. Development of subculture

42. A social worker is engaged in a one-on-one interview with a 10-year-old boy, in order to 42.____
    investigate allegations of a father's sexual abuse. The allegations were initially brought
    by the mother, now divorced from the father, and were later corroborated by the boy. The
    mother and father are engaged in a custody battle for the boy. The boy's account of
    events is extremely consistent over time, listing the same major events in sequence, but
    his affect is flat he relates his accounts of abuse in an oddly detached manner. The BEST
    action for the social worker at this point would be to

    A. terminate the interview and begin criminal proceedings against the father
    B. terminate the interview and refer the child for an immediate psychiatric consultation
    C. ask the mother to join in the interview and see if her account matches the boy's
    D. ask the boy to go into greater detail about the related events, out of sequence, and
       then repeat the request at a later time

43. When working with individuals or families of native American cultures, it is best to begin 43.____
    by

    A. gathering a social history
    B. using indirect approaches such as analogy or metaphor
    C. asking for open-ended descriptions of family roles
    D. direct questioning

44. In cases of elder abuse, the government may intervene if 44.____
    I. the older person requests it
    II. the older person is found at a hearing to be incompetent
    III. the abuse or neglect presents an unacceptable level of danger to the older
         person
    IV. the abuse is properly reported and recorded by a visiting social services
        worker

    A. I only
    B. I and II

C. I, II and III
D. I, II, III and IV

45. Which of the following is a guideline that should be observed in developing an assessment questionnaire for clients?

    A. Develop several focused questionnaires rather than a single all-purpose one.
    B. The most sensitive or probing questions should appear near the middle of the questionnaire.
    C. For complex ideas, form two-part questions.
    D. Include only open-ended questions.

46. During the assessment phase of an interview, checklists are most useful for identifying and selecting

    A. problems for intervention
    B. specific objectives
    C. available resources
    D. general goals

47. Which of the following is an advantage associated with the family life-cycle model?

    A. It highlights the special challenges of blended families.
    B. It identifies developmental tasks for families at specific stages.
    C. It is especially applicable to families in minority groups.
    D. It applies to those who do not have children.

48. Before making the decision to advocate on behalf of a client, it is important to consider several factors. Which of the following is NOT one of these?

    A. Client's consent for advocacy.
    B. Whether advocating is the most useful process that can be applied to the situation.
    C. Whether the complaint or decision involves a legitimate grievance
    D. Client's knowledge and feeling about human services.

49. Which of the following is an advantage associated with the use of genograms in client assessment?

    A. Targeting and identification of relevant social supports.
    B. Execution and interpretation require no instruction.
    C. Placement of an individual or family within a social context.
    D. A considerable shortening of the case record.

50. Activities involved in social casework typically include

    A. counseling those with a terminal illness
    B. supervising juvenile probation clients
    C. providing job training
    D. preparing court reports

51. In middle childhood, school-age children are generally concerned with

    A. "good" behavior in order to receive approval from others
    B. behaving appropriately because they fear punishment

C. the concordance of behaviors with an adopted moral code
D. conforming with group standards in order to be rewarded

52. When a social worker/client relationship is characterized by ineffectiveness, the most common reason is that

    A. resources are not available to meet the client's needs
    B. the client has not sufficiently specified his or her needs
    C. an incorrect solution has been identified by the worker
    D. the worker is attempting to keep the relationship on a pleasant level

53. A social history report includes the statement: "The subject claims to have completed high school." This should be included under the heading:

    A. Family Background and Situation
    B. Intellectual functioning
    C. Impressions and Assessment
    D. Such a statement shouldn't appear at all in a social history report.

54. According to Erickson, which of the following stages of psychosocial development occurs FIRST in the human life span?

    A. Initiative vs. guilt
    B. Trust vs. mistrust
    C. Identity vs. role confusion
    D. Autonomy vs. shame and doubt

55. The strategy of "reframing" is most useful for

    A. desensitizing clients to past trauma
    B. classifying client/family problems according to standard diagnostic categories
    C. helping clients to model their own behavior after others'
    D. revealing a client's strengths and opportunities for helping

56. In general, it is believed that interviewers who spend less than a minimum of _____ of an interview listening to the client are more active than they should be.

    A. one-fourth
    B. one-third
    C. one-half
    D. two thirds

57. In the _____ model of social work, the goal of the social worker is to enhance and restore the psychosocial functioning of persons, or to change noxious social conditions that impede the mutually beneficial interaction between person and their environment.

    A. structural-functional
    B. ecological
    C. medical
    D. strategic

58. In social work, "micro" practice usually focuses on

    A. resolving the problems of individuals, families, or small groups
    B. planning, administration, evaluation, and community organizing
    C. developmental activities in the social environment
    D. facilitating communication, mediation, and negotiation

59. _____ theory may prove most productive for the social work practitioner in understanding families of homosexuals, because it introduces unambiguous distinctions between stigma and homosexual behaviors and feelings.

    A. Structural
    B. Object relations
    C. Strategic
    D. Labeling

60. A client tells a practitioner that his main goal for intervention is to decide on a college major. To BEST help this client, the practitioner will assume the role of

    A. enabler
    B. mediator
    C. initiator
    D. educator

61. Which of the following is NOT a guideline for interacting with clients from a Latino culture?

    A. Efforts to foster independence and self-reliance may be interpreted by many Latinos as a lack of concern for others.
    B. Efforts to deal one-on-one with an adolescent client may serve to alienate the parents, especially the mother.
    C. A nonverbal gesture such as lowering the eyes is interpreted by many Latinos as a sign of respect and deference to authority.
    D. In much of Latino culture, the locus of control for problems tends to be much more external than internal.

62. The broadest, most general type of plan used in social work administration is the

    A. plan for meeting objectives
    B. statement of goals
    C. statement of mission
    D. guiding policies

63. In composing a social network grid with a client, which of the following steps is typically performed FIRST?

    A. Dividing acquaintances according to direction of help
    B. Dividing acquaintances according to duration of acquaintance
    C. Identifying people who can help the client in concrete ways
    D. Identifying areas of life in which people impact the client

64. An administrator notices, in several trips through the agency grounds, that a handful of the organization's support staff are often engaged in socializing or other nonproductive activities. The groups are always small and never made up of the same people, and nearly all members of the support staff have received satisfactory evaluations from their supervisor. The socializing does not occur around clients or visiting professionals. Over the past several years, the agency's efficiency record has remained about the same. The agency would probably be BEST served by the view that

   A. rigid controls should be implemented to reduce this behavior
   B. a memorandum should be circulated citing this behavior as a poor example
   C. the behavior may help to relieve boredom and should be ignored
   D. the supervisor should add an item or two to the evaluation that will address this behavior

65. Each of the following is a stage of the dying process described by Kübler-Ross, EXCEPT

   A. acknowledgement
   B. depression
   C. anger
   D. acceptance

66. For a prison inmate, "notice of rights" means the inmate
   I. receives advance notice of what conduct will result in discipline or punishment
   II. receives written notice of any charges against him
   III. is entitled to organize a group meeting for political purposes

   A. I and II
   B. I and III
   C. II and III
   D. I, II and III

67. Which of the following values is NOT generally indigenous to families of Asian heritage?

   A. Inconspicuousness
   B. Perfectionism
   C. Fatalism
   D. Shame as a behavioral influence

68. Most professionals recommend that in order to accurately evaluate the effect of an intervention, baseline data should be collected for no fewer than _____ data points.

   A. 2
   B. 3
   C. 4
   D. 5

69. During an assessment interview, a social worker and a client try to clarify and analyze the client's sense of self. If the worker wants to discover something about the client's self-acceptance, which of the following questions is MOST appropriate?

   A. To what extent do you worry about illness and physical incapacity?
   B. Is what you expect to happen mostly good or mostly bad?

C. Do you enjoy the times when you are alone?
D. Where do your other family members live?

70. Which of the following cognitive traits explains the mistaken belief held by many adolescents that they are invincible or protected from harmful consequences of their behavior?

    A. The personal fable
    B. Object delusion
    C. Egocentrism
    D. Pseudohypocrisy

71. An 18-year-old woman comes to see a social worker at a crisis center one day after being raped on a date. In the interview with this client, the social worker should FIRST:

    A. emphasize medical and legal procedures
    B. obtain factual information about the rape
    C. listen to the client and support her emotionally
    D. help the client establish contact with significant others

72. During a client assessment, each of the following should be considered a useful question, EXCEPT

    A. Can you tell me about times when you've successfully handled a problem like this in the past?
    B. When family members complain about your behavior, what to they say?
    C. How have you managed to cope up to this point?
    D. What do your friends and family seem to like most about you?

73. Norms are MOST accurately described as

    A. attitudes toward life events and processes
    B. assumptions about the world
    C. expectations of the self and others
    D. ideas about what is proper and desirable behavior

74. Generally, when a homeless person or group is removed from a condemned or abandoned property under the law, the most significant legal question to arise is whether

    A. the last owner of the property can be located for consent
    B. the property is being "rehabilitated" by the occupants
    C. the state recognizes a "right to shelter"
    D. the property has really been abandoned

75. A social worker introduces herself to a family household in which an elderly man lives. The man has been reported by neighbors on several occasions for making threats of violence to a number of adolescents in the neighborhood. The worker recognizes that she is uninvited, and the BEST way for her to describe the purpose of her relationship to the family would be as

A. helping the man to modify his behavior so that no further institutional involvement will be necessary
B. helping the man to avoid the aggravating stimulus of contact with neighborhood teens
C. protecting the neighborhood from the elderly man's threats
D. arranging for the man to get counseling in order to understand and change his behavior

---

KEY (CORRECT ANSWERS)

1. B	16. A	31. B	46. D	61. D
2. D	17. D	32. C	47. B	62. C
3. C	18. B	33. B	48. D	63. D
4. C	19. A	34. B	49. D	64. C
5. C	20. C	35. D	50. A	65. A
6. A	21. C	36. A	51. A	66. A
7. C	22. B	37. A	52. D	67. B
8. C	23. B	38. D	53. D	68. B
9. B	24. C	39. B	54. B	69. C
10. B	25. B	40. B	55. D	70. A
11. B	26. C	41. B	56. D	71. C
12. D	27. C	42. D	57. B	72. B
13. D	28. B	43. B	58. A	73. D
14. C	29. D	44. B	59. D	74. B
15. C	30. C	45. A	60. A	75. A

TEST 2

DIRECTIONS: Each question or incomplete statement is followed by several suggested answers or completions. Select the one that BEST answers the question or completes the statement. *PRINT THE LETTER OF THE CORRECT ANSWER IN THE SPACE AT THE RIGHT.*

1. A 24-year-old mother of four, recently widowed, tells a practitioner: "I feel like my whole life has just fallen apart. I don't think I can take care of my family on my own. My husband always made all the decisions and earned the money to support us. I haven't slept well since he died and I've started drinking more often. My parents try to help me but it's not enough."
   The practitioner responds by saying: "So you're afraid about your ability to shoulder all the family responsibilities now." This response is an example of a(n)

   A. reflection
   B. clarification
   C. paraphrase
   D. summarization

   1.____

2. At the beginning of an intake interview, a social worker's tasks are to
   I. gather data and conduct an assessment
   II. establish a positive relationship with the interviewee
   III. obtain brief details that will indicate whether the situation for which the client wants help is among the problems for which the worker offers help
   IV. offer help

   A. I only
   B. I and II
   C. II and III
   D. I, II, III and IV

   2.____

3. Which of the following is NOT a basic purpose of a professional code of ethics?

   A. To provide a mechanism for professional accountability
   B. To educate professionals about sound conduct
   C. To set standards that will be understood and enforced across all cultures
   D. To serve as a tool for improving practice

   3.____

4. According to cognitive-behavioral theory, schemas represent a client's

   A. subversive attempts to persist in faulty cognitions
   B. automatic responses
   C. different response patterns
   D. core beliefs and assumptions

   4.____

5. Objective data found in a client's folder might include

   A. A neighbor's recorded statement about a previous incident
   B. Notes on an interview with his psychotherapist
   C. A work evaluation performed by a supervisor
   D. A summary of previous criminal convictions

   5.____

6. In the middle phase of a client interview, as a problem is being further explored, the practitioner should spend a considerable amount of time

   A. interpreting behavior
   B. confronting discrepancies
   C. restating or paraphrasing
   D. negotiating a service contract

7. Which of the following statements is TRUE about social work assessment?

   A. It is another term for "goal setting."
   B. It identifies a problem and its potential impact.
   C. It refers to the search for alternative solutions.
   D. It relates to the evaluation of program effectiveness.

8. An agency needs to write a proposal to a private foundation in order to request funding for renovations. It will be necessary for the agency to organize a _____ group.

   A. training
   B. task-focused
   C. recreation
   D. self-help

9. Social exchange theory is based on the idea that people

   A. often attempt to superimpose their own needs onto the desires of others
   B. aim to protect themselves from punishment in relationships
   C. aim to maximize rewards and minimize costs in relationships
   D. exchange rewards with those who are most like themselves

10. Privileged communication typically applies in cases of
    I. marital infidelity, if both spouses are participating in treatment
    II. legal proceedings in which a practitioner is asked to produce client records in court
    III. child abuse or neglect
    IV. client disclosures of personal and sensitive information

    A. I and III
    B. I, II and IV
    C. III and IV
    D. I, II, III and IV

11. During an assessment interview, a practitioner asks questions about the client's customs and traditions. The practitioner is most likely seeking information about the impact of _____ on the client's functioning.

    A. unhealthy patterns
    B. self-talk
    C. interpersonal relationships
    D. cultural diversity

12. Each of the following is true of the intervention phase of social work, EXCEPT that it

    A. is focused on problems
    B. requires interviewing, recording, letter writing, and referral skills
    C. is guided by the principles of self-determination and acceptance
    D. results naturally from a thorough assessment

13. During a client interview, a practitioner is attempting to summarize what the client has just said, but the client gives signs that he does not agree with the summary and intends to interrupt. The practitioner believes it is important for the client to hear how the summary sounds in someone else's words. In order to maintain his turn at speaking, the practitioner may want to

    A. raise an index finger
    B. raise his eyebrows
    C. speak more loudly
    D. stop all accompanying gestures and body movements

14. In Erikson's model of human development, the stage at which a child learns to meet the demands of society is

    A. identity vs. role confusion
    B. industry vs. inferiority
    C. basic trust vs. mistrust
    D. autonomy vs. shame and doubt

15. Generally, controlled experimental designs account for about _____ percent of all social work research.

    A. 5
    B. 20
    C. 35
    D. 55

16. What is the term for a social work process that brings an intervention to a close?

    A. Recognizing success
    B. Integrating gains
    C. Terminating the relationship
    D. Expanding opportunities

17. Which of the following is an example of primary prevention for mental illness?

    A. Crisis intervention
    B. Parent-child communication training
    C. Psychotherapy
    D. Teacher referrals to social workers of children targeted by bullies

18. Which of the following is an example of a closed question?

    A. How do you think you can, as you've said, 'Come more alive?'
    B. Of all the problems we've discussed, which bothers you the most?
    C. What is your relationship with your family?
    D. What kinds of things do you find yourself longing for?

19. Over time, adult personalities are likely to change in each of the following ways, EXCEPT becoming more   19.____

    A. candid
    B. dependable
    C. receptive to the company of others
    D. accepting of hardship

20. Which of the following BEST describes the mission of social work?   20.____

    A. Meeting client needs while influencing social institutions to become more responsive to people
    B. Helping clients negotiate an often complex and difficult network of services
    C. Constantly responding and adapting to social changes in micro and macro environments
    D. Identifying programs and connecting clients to needed services

21. Numerous studies have been conducted to determine which factors in a client/helping professional relationship are consistently related to positive outcomes. Which of the following is/are NOT one of these conditions?   21.____

    A. A relationship analogous to doctor/patient
    B. Empathy and positive regard
    C. A working alliance
    D. Transference and countertransference

22. A person who donates anonymously to a favorite charity is most likely driven by what Maslow called   22.____

    A. intrinsic motivation
    B. extrinsic motivation
    C. affective habituation
    D. self-actualization

23. According to the NASW code of ethics, sexual contact between practitioners and former clients is   23.____

    A. strongly discouraged under any circumstances
    B. discouraged, but considered acceptable if it occurs two years or more after the professional relationship has been terminated
    C. grounds for expulsion from the social work profession
    D. a private matter whose nature is left entirely up to the practitioner and the client

24. During an unstructured interview with a client, a practitioner generally focuses on   24.____

    A. discovering the presenting problem
    B. confronting erroneous self-talk
    C. giving reflective responses that elicit more information
    D. a prescribed list of screening questions

25. Process recording is an assessment technique that is most often used in   25.____

    A. clinical settings
    B. family sculpting

C. one-on-one interviews
D. group sessions

26. The NASW's stance on bartering with clients, rather than simply charging fees for service, includes the opinion that social workers should
    I. participate in barter in only in very limited circumstances
    II. ensure that such arrangements are an accepted practice among professionals in the local community
    III. propose bartering if it is clear the client will be unable to pay for services
    IV. never barter with clients under any circumstances

    A. I only
    B. I and II
    C. I, II and III
    D. IV only

27. Etiquette, customs, and minor regulations are examples of

    A. mores
    B. norms
    C. ethics
    D. folkways

28. A practitioner working in the Adlerian model is likely to use each of the following as an assessment instrument, EXCEPT

    A. personality inventories
    B. ecomaps
    C. lifestyle inventories
    D. early childhood recollections

29. Which of the following information would typically be solicited at the LATEST point in an intake interview?

    A. educational history
    B. family/marital/sexual history
    C. vocational history
    D. past interventions or service requests

30. According to conflict theorists, the "hidden curriculum" of schools

    A. serves to transmit different cultural values
    B. encourages social integration
    C. often results in self-fulfilling prophecy
    D. perpetuates existing social inequalities

31. The high value placed on individual freedom in American society has arguably produced each of the following, EXCEPT

    A. a cultural paradox
    B. an environmental dilemma
    C. unfair economic competition
    D. a *caveat emptor* ("let the buyer beware") approach to the market economy

32. One model of the relationship between helping professionals and clients emphasizes the social influence of professionals in counseling roles. To be effective, practitioners in the counseling role can draw on a power base that arises out of the relationship with the client. In client relationships, the power base that is typically LEAST helpful for the practitioner is known as _____ power.

    A. referent
    B. expert
    C. legitimate
    D. reward

33. In social work, experimental research designs

    A. are the most commonly conducted form of social work research
    B. obligate the researcher to offer a treatment to a control group as soon as possible after the study is terminated
    C. are usually single-system designs
    D. are generally free of ethical concerns if the research is conducted well

34. The term "social stratification" refers to social inequality that is

    A. differential
    B. structured
    C. institutionally sanctioned
    D. imperceptible

35. To a practitioner working from the behavioral perspective, the most important feature of good relationships is

    A. effective coping behaviors
    B. freedom from conflict
    C. complementary needs
    D. well-established boundaries

36. In an initial interview, it is common for clients to

    A. break down emotionally
    B. describe problems in a way that minimizes their own contributions to them
    C. disclose very personal information and emotions
    D. be someone other than the person who has arranged the interview

37. Which of the following is NOT a trend in the use of family approaches in direct social work practice?

    A. Increased attention on the family as an isolated system
    B. Increased attention to family diversity
    C. The use of a variety of social science theoretical approaches
    D. The use of multiple intervention models

38. The process whereby a client's place past feelings or attitudes toward significant people in their lives onto their social work practitioner is known as

    A. transference
    B. denial

C. countertransference
D. projection

39. Social desirability bias often causes people to

    A. make appraisals of others that are based on their social functioning rather than their effectiveness in other roles
    B. attribute their successes to skill, while blaming external factors for failures
    C. modify their responses to surveys or interviews based on what they think are desirable responses
    D. focus on the style of their interactions with others, rather than the substance

40. A social worker attends an evening anniversary party at which she has consumed some alcohol, which she rarely drinks. She doesn't think she is literally drunk, but would acknowledge feeling slightly tipsy and perhaps not in full command of herself. When she arrives at home later, she listens to a message from a client that was left on her answering machine while she was out. The client, with whom she has met several times, is feeling lonely and desperate because of the recent loss of his wife to cancer. The social worker wants to help. She should

    A. return the call immediately and try to counsel the client
    B. return the call immediately and explain that she is unable to help right now, but will call first thing tomorrow
    C. avoid contacting the client until she has recovered her ability to perform up to her usual professional standards and judgement
    D. contact a trusted colleague, give him or her the relevant information, and ask that he or she try to counsel the client over the phone

41. During an assessment interview, a practitioner asks a client: "What kinds of feelings do you have when this happens to you?" The practitioner is trying to identify the _____ associated with the problem.

    A. affect and mood states
    B. secondary gains
    C. overt behaviors or motoric responses
    D. internal dialogue

42. Hospital social workers typically engage in each of the following types of interventions or practice, EXCEPT

    A. crisis intervention
    B. discharge planning
    C. long-term counseling
    D. group work

43. For social work practitioners, symptoms of "burnout" on the job typically include each of the following, EXCEPT

    A. feeling unable to accomplish goals
    B. emotional exhaustion
    C. chronic worry
    D. a feeling of detachment from clients and work

44. When a case manager reaches the point in service coordination during which he makes a referral, he has assumed the role of

    A. evaluator
    B. broker
    C. advocate
    D. planner

45. A practitioner encounters a situation in which his own personal values conflict with a client's. In this instance, the practitioner is expected to engage in

    A. peer review
    B. value suspension
    C. legal consultation
    D. value clarification

46. Among the following American groups, the women who have the greatest risk of HIV infection are

    A. white
    B. African American
    C. Native American
    D. Hispanic

47. The trend in school social work has been a gradual shift toward an emphasis on the _____ perspective.

    A. behavioral
    B. input-based
    C. ecological
    D. psychiatric

48. The success of client-written logs as an assessment tool may depend on the client's motivation to keep a log. Which of the following is LEAST likely to help motivate a client to keep a log?

    A. Establishing a clear rationale or purpose for keeping the log
    B. Establishing negative consequences if the client fails to make log entries
    C. Adapting the log type to the client's abilities to self-monitor
    D. Involving the client in discussing and analyzing the log

49. The social work value of *empathy* is defined as a practitioner's capacity to

    A. imagine oneself in another's situation
    B. feel compassion for a person who is in distress
    C. convince a person that things will get better
    D. make a person recognize his/her own inner strength

50. Focusing on a client's positive assets and strengths during an assessment interview
    I. emphasizes the wholeness of the client system, rather than simply the problematic aspects
    II. gives a practitioner information about potential problems that might arise during an intervention
    III. helps convey to the client that they have internal resources that may prove useful
    IV. risks skewing the effectiveness of an intervention by taking the focus off the presenting problem

    A. I and III
    B. I, II and III
    C. III only
    D. I, II, III and IV

51. A hospital social worker is meeting with an 86-year-old man who suffers from Alzheimer's disease. His symptoms thus far have consisted largely of incidents of forgetfulness, and he has shown no signs of dementia or violence. The client's daughter, who has recently succeeded in having her father grant her a power of attorney over his affairs. When the social worker asks questions of the client, the daughter repeated breaks in and attempts to answer for him, though he appears to be lucid. When the social worker asks to speak to the client alone, the daughter refuses. The social worker should

    A. suspect a case of elder abuse and contact the adult protective services agency to look into it
    B. pretend to leave, and then attempt to interview the man when the daughter leaves the room
    C. suspect that the daughter may have suffered abuse at the hands of her father and adult protective services to look into it
    D. suspect a case of elder abuse and contact local law enforcement authorities

52. Which of the following is a key element of the case management paradigm?

    A. A focus on improving the quality and accessibility of resources
    B. A focus on developing vocational adjustment
    C. The selection of interventions based on empirical research
    D. Rational-emotive therapy

53. Of the following health problems, each affects the elderly to a greater extent than other age groups. The one that leads by the greatest percentage is

    A. cancer
    B. stroke
    C. heart disease
    D. Alzheimer's disease

54. Approximately _____ of all direct practice interventions are terminated because of unanticipated situational factors.

    A. an eighth
    B. a quarter
    C. half
    D. three-quarters

55. Social factors that increase the risk for suicide include each of the following, EXCEPT that the person

   A. lives alone
   B. has repeatedly rejected support
   C. has no ongoing therapeutic relationship
   D. is married

56. Practitioners are generally considered to have an ethical obligation to do each of the following, EXCEPT

   A. remain aware of their own values
   B. seek to learn about the diverse cultural backgrounds of their clients
   C. avoid imposing their values on clients
   D. refer clients whose values strongly differ from their own

57. Studies of young people who join urban gangs suggests that most often, people join gangs because of a need for a(n)

   A. peer group
   B. outlet for pent-up aggression and frustration
   C. surrogate family
   D. vehicle for criminal activity

58. After terminating a working relationship with a social worker, a client joins the local chapter of Alcoholics Anonymous. In doing so, she is attempting to

   A. form new therapeutic relationships
   B. prolong treatment
   C. maintain gains
   D. generalize gains

59. A key concept of narrative therapy is the idea tha

   A. clients often construct one-dimensional stories that don't tell the whole truth
   B. clearly naming a problem or disorder is the first step in solving it
   C. problems are inseparable from the person
   D. interventions are narrowly targeted to "revisions" of specific passages within the story

60. The creation of social service programs typically accomplishes each of the following, EXCEPT

   A. prevention
   B. enhancement
   C. retrenchment
   D. remediation

61. The most significant health problem facing Native Americans today is

   A. tuberculosis
   B. alcoholism
   C. heart disease
   D. diabetes

62. Which of the following is NOT one of the six "core values" that is cited in the preamble to the NASW's code of ethics?

    A. Service
    B. Confidentiality
    C. Integrity
    D. Importance of human relationships

63. Each of the following is a guideline for a practitioner's participation in crisis intervention procedures, EXCEPT

    A. expressing empathy by saying things such as "I understand"
    B. asking the client to describe the event
    C. letting the client talk for as long as he or she likes without interruption
    D. asking the client to describe his or her reactions and responses

64. A practitioner has begun to work with clients in one-on-one settings. He thinks perhaps self-disclosure would be a good way to establish a solid, caring relationship with his clients. He should remember that in working with clients professionally, there will always be a tension between the competing forces of self-disclosure and

    A. candor
    B. liability
    C. reciprocity
    D. privacy

65. From an ethical standpoint, practitioners may
    I. accept a referral fee
    II. refer a client to a single referral source
    III. use a place of employment, such as a social services agency, to recruit clients for their own private practice
    IV. refer clients only if their problems fall outside the practitioner's area of competence

    A. I and II
    B. II only
    C. II, III and IV
    D. I, II, III and IV

66. According to Carol H. Meyer's widely used model of social work assessment, the first step in the assessment process is

    A. evaluation
    B. inferential thinking
    C. problem definition
    D. exploration

67. What is the term for the theory that explains how people generate explanations for the behaviors of others?

    A. Attribution theory
    B. Stereotyping

C. Thematic apperception
D. Implicit personality theory

68. The most important professional risk associated with amalgamating groups under very broad headings or labels, such as "Asian American," is that

    A. these terms are considered derogatory by many people
    B. most immigrants to this country proudly insist on being referred to as simply "American"
    C. many people resent being folded in to a larger group for the purpose of classification
    D. the label may obscure significant differences in the culture and experiences of individuals or subgroups within the larger category

68.____

69. Before entering a social work field placement program, prospective students are ethically entitled to know
    I. dismissal policies and procedures
    II. employment prospects for graduates
    III. the basis for performance evaluation
    IV. names and theoretical perspectives of prospective supervisors

    A. I only
    B. I, II, and III
    C. III only
    D. I, II, III and IV

69.____

70. Of the steps involved in recruitment and training at human services organizations, the FIRST typically involves

    A. reference and background checks
    B. posting position announcements
    C. screening interviews
    D. developing a job description

70.____

71. During an intake interview, a client generally avoids making eye contact with the practitioner. Averting the eyes in this way is an example of the _____ function of eye contact.

    A. monitoring
    B. expressive
    C. regulatory
    D. cognitive

71.____

72. The educational success of American children and youth is highly correlated to

    A. home schooling
    B. regional employment patterns
    C. family values
    D. race and ethnicity

72.____

73. Which of the following techniques is a client-centered practitioner MOST likely to use?

    A. Response shaping
    B. Reflection

73.____

C. Giving advice
D. Analysis

74. During a meeting with a client who has just ended his marriage after twelve years, the client insists repeatedly that everything is fine. No matter what the practitioner asks or tries to suggest, the response is the same. The client is engaging in the facial management technique known as

   A. neutralizing
   B. masking
   C. intensifying
   D. deintensifying

75. A practitioner is considering a dual relationship with a client. Before forming such a relationship, the practitioner should consider
   I. divergent responsibilities
   II. incompatible expectations
   III. the power differential
   IV. referring the client to another practitioner

   A. I and II
   B. I, II and III
   C. II, III and IV
   D. I, II, III and IV

KEY (CORRECT ANSWERS)

1. A	16. B	31. A	46. B	61. B
2. C	17. B	32. D	47. C	62. B
3. C	18. B	33. B	48. B	63. A
4. D	19. C	34. B	49. A	64. D
5. D	20. A	35. A	50. B	65. B
6. C	21. A	36. B	51. A	66. D
7. B	22. A	37. A	52. A	67. A
8. B	23. A	38. A	53. C	68. D
9. C	24. C	39. C	54. C	69. B
10. B	25. C	40. C	55. D	70. D
11. D	26. B	41. A	56. D	71. C
12. A	27. D	42. C	57. C	72. D
13. C	28. A	43. C	58. C	73. B
14. B	29. B	44. B	59. A	74. A
15. A	30. D	45. B	60. C	75. B

EXAMINATION SECTION

TEST 1

DIRECTIONS: Each question or incomplete statement is followed by several suggested answers or completions. Select the one that BEST answers the question or completes the statement. *PRINT THE LETTER OF THE CORRECT ANSWER IN THE SPACE AT THE RIGHT.*

1. The one of the following which is the PRINCIPAL medium of casework service is
    A. skilled diagnosis and realistic treatment planning
    B. personal communication or relationship established between the client and the worker
    C. agency organization in relation to program objectives
    D. the combined knowledge, skill, and attitude of the worker

    1._____

2. Treatment aimed at helping the client maintain his adaptive pattern is directed toward
    A. alleviating undue pressures in the client's everyday life and strengthening his emotional reactions to psychological pressure
    B. modifying the client's unrealistic life pattern by confronting him with explanations for his behavior
    C. assuming a passive role in order to avoid disturbing the client's adjustment
    D. working with those aspects of the client's problems which are related to environmental factors

    2._____

3. On account of the multi-faceted and dynamic nature of clients' problems, of the following, it is NECESSARY for the social worker to
    A. analyze the total problem before proceeding with treatment
    B. develop a comprehensive treatment plan which approaches the main aspects of the total problem
    C. separate the personality and behavioral aspects of the problem from the social setting
    D. select some part of the problem as the unit for work

    3._____

4. The one of the following which is the MOST important consideration in evaluating the ego strength of an angry, deprived, mistreated, frustrated, evasive client is the client's ability to
    A. verbalize his problems to someone
    B. redirect his anger towards an object
    C. form a relationship with an accepting worker
    D. hold a job

    4._____

5. When a client is torn between choices that immobilize him or make his problem less manageable, the social worker should base his practice with the client on the following, with the EXCEPTION of
    A. identification of the client's problem
    B. persuading the client to act according to his instructions
    C. determination with the client of preferred approaches in dealing with the problem
    D. enabling the client to take constructive action to deal with the problem

5._____

6. Assume that a social worker reports that a mother with whom she is working claims that the school is discriminating against her children because she is a welfare recipient. Her children have a history of truancy and poor school achievement. The worker feels that the mother's assessment of the situation has some validity.
Of the following, the BEST course of action for the worker to take is to
    A. support the mother's defense of her children and report the alleged discrimination by the school to the Board of Education
    B. inquire further into the reasons for the children's truancy and poor achievement with the children, the mother, and school officials
    C. explore with the mother her feelings about receiving public assistance, and encourage her to find a job so she won't need assistance
    D. disengage herself from her close involvement in this case since she has stopped being objective

6._____

7. A social worker has as a client a 17-year-old boy who is part of a group whose norm of behavior is cutting classes, frequent absenteeism, sexual promiscuity, and petty thievery. He wants to finish school and to grow up, but the present peer-group pressure militates against this, and he is damaging his values by following the group's norms.
The social worker would be MOST helpful to this boy if, of the following, he takes the role of a
    A. mediator, to help support the boy against the demands of the group, and also to give him direct help in defending himself psychologically
    B. resource person, to refer the boy to a youth agency that would be able to work with the boy in his peer group
    C. interpreter, to help the boy realize the inappropriateness of his behavior in the peer group
    D. peer model, to help the boy identify with a young, successful person

7._____

8. A fifteen-year-old boy has been referred to a social worker with a history of arrests for repeated acts of minor delinquency, suspension from school for truancy, and a hostile attitude towards treatment. He is financially supported by his parents, but they seem to have stopped giving him emotional support and say that he is uncontrollable.
The boy's interests would be served BEST if, of the following, the social worker's role were that of
   A. psychosocial counselor using traditional insight development
   B. educator in teaching the boy the skills he would need to succeed
   C. catalyst in family therapy, to help the boy and his parents handle their feelings and the reality problems constructively
   D. crisis intervenor, taking an assertive role to give direction and specific help

9. The one of the following which is a COMMON error made by new social workers who are beginning to find out about the influence of unconscious desires and emotions on human behavior is to
   A. probe the client unnecessarily
   B. become over-assured that they can solve the client's problem
   C. slow up the pace of the interview
   D. look for the proper treatment method based on the client's neuroses

10. Although we can judge statements about objective verifiable matters to be true or false, we are not similarly justified in passing judgment on subjective attitudes.
Of the following, this statement BEST explains the rationale behind the social work principle of
   A. empathy
   B. abreaction
   C. non-judgmentality
   D. confidentiality

11. The one of the following which BEST describes the meaning of ambivalence in social work is: The
   A. social worker refrains from imposing his moral judgments on the client
   B. supervisor assists the worker in understanding the psychological causes for the client's behavior
   C. client is seeking someone who will understand the subjective reasons for his behavior
   D. client has conflicting interests, desires, and emotions

12. The CORRECT definition of the term *acceptance* as used in social work is as follows:
   A. A decision made at intake to accept the client as a case for the agency to handle
   B. The concept of a positive and active understanding by the worker of the feelings a client expresses through his behavior
   C. The concept that the worker does not pass judgment on the client's behavior
   D. Communication to the client that the worker does not condone and accept his antisocial behavior

13. Psychiatrists are usually concerned with the total functioning and integration of the human personality.
    Of the following, social workers USUALLY concentrate on
    A. the same thing but for shorter periods of time
    B. the same thing but without prescribing medication
    C. helping the client to deal with the presenting problem
    D. making the proper referrals to assist the client in dealing with his problem

14. The one of the following which is a DESCRIPTIVE term for a client who is resistive, breaks appointments, withholds information, beclouds issues, related to others in a primitive, often distorted fashion, and acts out his wishes and conflicts in his contact with the worker is
    A. psychotic
    B. manic depressive
    C. paranoid schizophrenic
    D. character disorder

15. The one of the following which is a MAJOR reason why it is so difficult for social workers to exert influence on social policy is:
    A. Social workers are trained to implement existing policies, not to change those that are unworkable
    B. Those who make policy are influenced by numerous forces, persons, values, and aspirations, not all of which relate directly to the policy decisions to be made
    C. As a result of the heavy concentration on casework in the graduate schools, most social workers put more emphasis on working with individuals, rather than on social policy
    D. Psychological and psychiatric concepts are disputed by experts in the field, so that it is difficult to diagnose motives

16. The one of the following which is the BEST explanation of the rationale of *crisis intervention* as a treatment method is:
    A. A little help, rationally directed and purposefully focused at an extremely critical time in the client's life, can be more effective than more extensive help given during a less critical period
    B. Because clients are more likely to react precipitously at times of crisis, social workers must give particular emphasis at such times to providing direct and aggressive advice and assistance
    C. The social worker should make full use of the client's vulnerable emotional state at a time of crisis in order to bring him face to face with his defense mechanisms and with the realities of life
    D. The client's urgent need for emotional support at times of crisis should be used by the social worker at such times to gain the client's confidence and trust

17. In establishing contact with a new, unfamiliar group, of the following, the group worker's usual FIRST action should be to
    A. discuss the sponsoring agency and its function
    B. give special attention to the less aggressive members
    C. reinforce the authority of the natural group leader
    D. approach the group at their own level of language and interests

18. If a group worker should become aware that some members of his group feel resentful toward him, of the following, it would GENERALLY be advisable for the worker to
    A. make a special effort to please the resentful members
    B. offer to resign from leadership of the group
    C. attempt to convey to the resentful members his own attitude of acceptance of them
    D. enlist the support of other group members to convince the resentful ones of his good intentions

19. Assume that, during the sixth weekly session of activity group therapy with a group of adolescent boys, they engage in horseplay, use obscene language, and become quite uncontrollable.
    Of the following, it can SAFELY be concluded that the
    A. boys are testing the worker to learn his limits of tolerance
    B. worker's status as the group leader is being seriously challenged
    C. composition of the group should be changed
    D. worker should end the session and dismiss the boys

20. Of the following, the role of the group worker at meetings of a group which has its own officers is to
    A. withdraw from the activities of the group
    B. make decisions for the group if required
    C. clarify issues and teach skills when necessary
    D. handle hostile or aggressive members

21. Schizophrenia in children USUALLY becomes manifest
    A. during the latency period
    B. during adolescence only
    C. when the mother has a history of schizophrenia
    D. during early childhood or adolescence

22. Sickle cell anemia is a blood disease MOST commonly found in children whose parents are
    A. Caucasian   B. interracial
    B. black or Latin American   D. oriental

23. A decline in hearing and vision takes place in healthy persons during the period BEGINNING at age
    A. 30   B. 40   C. 50   D. 60

24. The MOST common complaint made by psychiatric patients is concerned with
    A. depression   B. panic   C. insomnia   D. fatigue

25. The one of the following which is *most likely* to cause the reappearance in old age of a previously compensated neurosis is
    A. decrease in social status, loss of persons and possessions or presence of injuries and illnesses
    B. decrease in sensory and cognitive capacities resulting in poor reality testing
    C. cerebro-arteriosclerosis or other cerebrovascular disturbance
    D. decrease in financial resources, resulting in heightened anxiety

25._____

KEY (CORRECT ANSWERS)

1. B
2. A
3. D
4. C
5. B

6. B
7. A
8. C
9. A
10. C

11. D
12. B
13. C
14. D
15. B

16. A
17. D
18. C
19. A
20. C

21. D
22. C
23. B
24. A
25. A

TEST 2

DIRECTIONS: Each question or incomplete statement is followed by several suggested answers or completions. Select the one that BEST answers the question or completes the statement. *PRINT THE LETTER OF THE CORRECT ANSWER IN THE SPACE AT THE RIGHT.*

1. Of the following, group approaches are COMMONLY used for
    A. encounter, discussion, training, and administration
    B. education, counseling, therapy, and recreation
    C. counseling, recreation, catharsis, and crisis intervention
    D. counseling, leadership, administration, and training

    1._____

2. The purposes of group counseling are the following, with the EXCEPTION of
    A. avoidance of treating pathology as such
    B. helping clients attain a better level of functioning
    C. modifying social and familial problems
    D. resolving intra-psychic conflicts

    2._____

3. The separation of public assistance recipients into categories had its origins in the
    A. Elizabethan poor law
    B. numerous amendments to the Social Security Act
    C. legislation of the Massachusetts Bay Colony
    D. Social Security Act of 1935

    3._____

4. The one of the following which is the FIRST form of social insurance to be widely developed in the United States is
    A. workmen's compensation or industrial accident insurance
    B. unemployment insurance programs
    C. temporary disability insurance
    D. old age insurance for industrial workers

    4._____

5. The doctrine of less eligibility, which has been considered over the years as a policy for public assistance programs, means most nearly that
    A. grants should always be below subsistence level in order to give recipients an incentive to seek employment
    B. eligibility for public assistance should be established on the basis of a limited number of basic budgetary needs
    C. income derived from public assistance benefits should not exceed the amount earned by the lowest paid independent worker in the community
    D. categories of need should be established in each community and ranked in order of priority in order to determine eligibility for assistance

    5._____

6. Social insurance programs such as OASDHI and unemployment insurance have been CRITICIZED widely because, of the following,
   a. there is an inherent conflict between the intent to prevent poverty on the one hand, and wage-relatedness of the programs on the other
   b. there is no relationship between the amount or the benefits and differences in cost of living in various localities within a state
   c. the programs do not include review of personal and family problems
   d. a large percentage of the grants go to persons who are otherwise financially able to support themselves

7. The one of the following which would be the basis of a family allowance plan SIMILAR to programs in effect in Canada and France is:
   a. Family size, for all needy families with minor children whose current annual income is below specified levels
   b. The total number of persons in the household, including all adults except those receiving social security benefits
   c. The number of minor children, available to all families and requiring no means test
   d. Income level, available to all families with minor children

8. A MAJOR criticism of social and health programs as they exist today has been the tendency towards a *problem focus* rather than a *social goals* approach.
   Of the following, this approach has resulted in
   a. a lack of an integrated, systematic development of programs that deal adequately with social and health problems
   b. excessive expenditures for the social and health problems that have received the most attention, at the expense of other equally serious problems
   c. a federal and nationwide approach rather than the more desirable *geographic approach*, which would bring delivery of services closer to the people
   d. the development of legislation which shows little evidence of recognition of the contributions that could be made by social planners

9. A striking feature of American culture is its tendency to identify standards of personal excellence with competitive occupational achievement.
   The one of the following which is the CONSEQUENCE of this feature for those unable to make one's own living through work is to
   a. increase incentive to find a productive job
   b. lower the individual's feeling of self-worth and generate a feeling of powerlessness
   c. give the individual a need to control the environment
   d. encourage increased educational attainment

10. Of the following, the objectives and curriculum content of graduate schools of social work today GENERALLY indicate an *increased* emphasis on
    a. prevention and institutional change in addition to treatment
    b. knowledge of individual personality factors and treatment methods
    c. the separate methods and goals of classroom study and field work
    d. the use of the one-to-one instructor-student relationship for both classroom study and field work

10._____

11. At present, there is a general consensus among social welfare educators and administrators that not every job requires a professional social worker with a master's degree in social work.
    The one of the following which is the MOST important reason for this viewpoint is that personnel with lower educational qualifications can
    a. be used as a valuable temporary expedient for jobs that would otherwise remain unfilled
    b. perform certain social work tasks as well or even better than workers with master's degrees
    c. gain experience that will spur them on to attend a graduate school of social work in order to obtain the degree
    d. be used to reduce substantially personnel costs in public and private social work agencies

11._____

12. In an era of rapid change, of the following, the REAL test of the social work profession is to
    a. meet constructively the demands of that change
    b. hold to its traditional practices
    c. abandon its methods for new approaches
    d. wait to see what happens to other professions

12._____

13. The psychologist who is USUALLY associated with a theory of self-psychology which has as its basic concept the assertion that a man has a tendency to actualize himself, i.e., to maintain and improve himself, is
    A. Karl Jung   B. Sigmund Freud
    C. B.F. Skinner   D. Carl Rogers

13._____

14. Of the types of mental breakdown listed below, the disorder that ordinarily occurs at the MOST advanced age is
    A. cerebral arteriosclerosis
    B. neurasthenia
    C. dementia praecox
    D. paresis

14._____

15. Principles of crisis intervention in social casework have been derived LARGELY from the theoretical formulations of
    a. Harry Stack Sullivan and Clara Thompson
    b. August P. Hollingshead and Frederick C. Redlich
    c. Otto Rank and Jessie Taft
    d. Erich Lindemann and Gerald Caplan

15._____

16. Of the following, the MOST important reason that those responsible for the care of a child in placement should *never* depreciate the child's natural parents or the home from which he came is that the
    a. child's self-esteem depends on how he feels about his natural parents and his previous experiences
    b. natural parents may have been incapable of being adequate parents
    c. child may feel the substitute parents are jealous of his natural parents
    d. child will be forced into the position of defending his natural parents and will resent the substitute parents

17. Although day care was originally established mainly as a social service for working mothers, it has been found that, of the following,
    a. working mothers of physically and mentally handicapped children do not benefit from day care facilities
    b. most working mothers would prefer to leave their children with friends or relatives rather than at a day care center
    c. it would be economically feasible and beneficial for communities to establish day care centers which would be available to all mothers in the community
    d. day care can also be an educational experience for a child and be helpful in the development of peer relationships

18. Research studies of language development in young children have shown that, of the following,
    a. the multiple mothering of children in a large family retards language development
    b. language retardation in otherwise normal children is usually related to inadequate language stimulation
    c. language retardation is always associated with slow motor development
    d. children are usually slow in learning to talk when more than one language is spoken in the home

19. The *battered child syndrome* is reported to be one of the most difficult problems facing health officials. When a worker knows of a case of a child being severely physically abused, of the following, he SHOULD
    a. get psychiatric consultation to understand the parents' motives
    b. advise the child to stay away from the parents
    c. help the parents to see what they're doing is wrong
    d. report the case to child protective authorities

20. The one of the following which is a *psychological principle* which can BEST be described as a situation in which an individual experiences some ambivalence and indecisiveness in choosing one or more desired objects or goals is
    A. task-orientation B. conflict
    C. apathy D. projection

21. The *treatment method* which allows or encourages the client to express his charged feelings around a pressing emotional need is known as
    A. exploring
    B. synthesizing
    C. catharsis
    D. ventilating

21._____

22. The *emotional release* that results from recall of a previously forgotten painful experience is known as
    A. introjection
    B. abreaction
    C. sublimation
    D. free association

22._____

23. The *action* whereby an individual directs his aggression against an innocent bystander rather than expressing it against the source of his difficulties, is called
    A. displacement
    B. projection
    C. introjection
    D. abreaction

23._____

24. An *attempt* to attribute emotionally caused behavior to reasonable factors MORE acceptable to the individual is known as
    A. projection
    B. rationalization
    C. introjection
    D. free association

24._____

25. The UNCONSCIOUS *application* of elements of the experiences in a former relationship to a new relationship is known as
    A. projection
    B. abreaction
    C. transference
    D. sublimation

25._____

KEY (CORRECT ANSWERS)

1. B	11. B
2. D	12. A
3. A	13. D
4. A	14. A
5. C	15. D
6. A	16. A
7. C	17. D
8. A	18. B
9. B	19. D
10. A	20. B

21. D
22. B
23. A
24. B
25. C

EXAMINATION SECTION
TEST 1

DIRECTIONS: Each question or incomplete statement is followed by several suggested answers or completions. Select the one that BEST answers the question or completes the statement. *PRINT THE LETTER OF THE CORRECT ANSWER IN THE SPACE AT THE RIGHT.*

1. An engaged couple is seeing a social worker for premarital counseling. The woman reports that her fiance's family doesn't accept her because of her religion, and she doesn't want to convert. Her fiance agrees that this is a problem and that he is "torn" between his parents and his wife-to-be. The social worker should FIRST:

    A. discuss ways the couple can help his parents accept their relationship
    B. explore the impact of this issue on their relationship
    C. focus on how they plan to handle their religious differences when they are married
    D. recommend individual sessions for each to deal with their feelings

2. A single parent of two small children is being seen for an intake interview at a family service agency. She begins to cry when describing her pressures and stresses, and the decisions she is facing since the sudden death of her husband three months ago. She apologizes to the worker for "acting like a baby" and says she knows that her problems could be worse. The social worker should FIRST:

    A. suggest that the client prioritize her problems
    B. help the client identify her coping mechanisms
    C. suggest a referral to a bereavement group
    D. acknowledge the difficulty of dealing with numerous problems

3. Which of the following factors is NOT used in establishing a diagnosis using the DSM-IV?

    A. Physical functioning
    B. Psychosocial stressors
    C. Clinical syndromes
    D. Medical conditions

4. A couple in their mid-thirties seek marital counseling from a social worker because they have been experiencing conflict over their sexual relationship. The wife reports that she feels emotionally detached from her husband. They decided early in their marriage not to have children, and both are involved and committed to their careers. The social worker should focus on the couple's:

    A. career objectives
    B. parenting decision
    C. sexual relationship
    D. relationship issues

5. A couple comes to a family service agency requesting help in communicating better with each other. The social worker should FIRST:

A. engage the couple in a discussion of male/female communication patterns
B. facilitate role-playing of effective and dysfunctional communication techniques
C. explore what the couple means by better communication
D. gather psychosocial background information on each client, including marital history

6. Which of the following statements is **NOT** true when a social work agency employs a consultant?

    A. The consultant's role need not be sanctioned by the agency's administration.
    B. The consultant's role rests primarily on specialized knowledge and skill.
    C. Consultation is an indirect means of influencing skills of agency staff.
    D. The ultimate beneficiary of consultation is the agency clientele.

7. When a client's behavior is particularly resistant to extinction, the behavior is likely to have been maintained in the past by:

    A. consistent reinforcement
    B. consistent punishment
    C. intermittent reinforcement
    D. intermittent punishment

8. According to the DSM-IV, which of the following symptoms is **NOT** associated with a diagnosis of schizophrenia?

    A. Delusions
    B. Flight of ideas
    C. Affectional flattening
    D. Disorganized speech

9. A six-year-old exhibits repetitive whole-body movements, gross deficits in language development, and a lack of emotional responsiveness. The social worker suspects a diagnosis of:

    A. post-traumatic stress disorder
    B. organic brain syndrome
    C. attention-deficit/hyperactivity disorder
    D. autistic disorder

10. To attempt to extinguish a child's talking to himself in class, a social worker using a behavior modification approach will **FIRST**:

    A. determine how frequently the child talks to himself in class
    B. meet with the child individually and ask to whom he is talking
    C. include the child in a group for children with delayed social skills
    D. remove the child from the class each time he begins talking to himself

11. A client is being seen for symptoms of depression and anxiety, but has been resistant to efforts to refer her for a medication evaluation. The client states that medication is a "crutch" and she should be able to solve her problems without it. During a session following a very upsetting weekend, the client cries and says that she will see "a shrink for pills that will solve her problems." In facilitating the client's referral to the psychiatrist, the social worker should **FIRST**:

A. give the client a list of recommended psychiatrists
B. phone for a psychiatric appointment while the client is still in the office
C. discuss the client's expectation of the consultation
D. suggest the client review her insurance coverage

12. A mother has been referred to a family service agency after learning that her 14-year-old son is diabetic, because of the son's denial of the illness by "forgetting" to test his blood sugar and take insulin as directed. When she asks him how he is feeling, he tells her either to leave him alone or "chill out." The mother bursts into tears, saying she is a "nervous wreck," and worries about her son constantly. The social worker should FIRST:

    A. reassure the mother that her son's reactions are typical adolescent responses
    B. explore family and community resources available to the mother
    C. acknowledge the mother's feelings of fear and apprehension
    D. suggest that a joint interview with mother and son be scheduled

13. The MOST difficult aspect of conducting a cost-benefit analysis is:

    A. determining the units of services
    B. enumerating interventions
    C. establishing a control group
    D. operationally defining outcomes

14. Which of the following statistical tests is a nonparametric test of significance?

    A. Analysis of variance
    B. T-test
    C. Pearson's r
    D. Chi-square

15. A social work manager in a hospital setting decides to establish an interdisciplinary collaborative team to review advanced directive procedures. The FIRST step in this process is to:

    A. identify the areas of expertise needed on the team
    B. identify the persons to be assigned to the team
    C. select the leader of the proposed team
    D. develop a rationale for the inclusion of a social worker

16. The desire for control and perfection is characteristic of which of the following personality disorders?

    A. Borderline
    B. Narcissistic
    C. Obsessive-compulsive
    D. Antisocial

17. After four months of treatment, a client informs his social worker that he has received a job transfer to another city and will move the following week. The social worker should FIRST:

A. review with the client progress made and treatment goals not yet achieved
B. discuss with the client his reasons for not informing the social worker of his plans to move sooner
C. ask the client to sign a release of information form in case he wants to enter treatment at a later time
D. advise the client to become involved in treatment as soon as possible in the new city

18. A social work staff is experiencing an increasing number of clients who fail to keep their appointments. All of the following administrative interventions are appropriate **EXCEPT**:

    A. scheduling a meeting with the staff members to assess their views of the problem
    B. sending a questionnaire to all of the clients who have failed to keep their appointments over the last month
    C. informing clients that they will be charged for not canceling appointments they are unable to keep
    D. terminating clients who do not keep their appointments

19. A five-year-old is scheduled for open heart surgery. Part of the procedure for the operation involves catheterization and an incision in the child's groin. The procedure has been explained to him. He responded to the idea of heart surgery with little or no anxiety but has extreme concern about the catheterization. From a psychodynamic point of view, his anxiety stems from fear of:

    A. mutilation
    B. separation
    C. annihilation
    D. pain

20. A man was referred by his attorney to a social worker after he was charged with sexually molesting a minor. The case is scheduled for trial. The goal of the social worker in treating this client should be to:

    A. gather information in order to prepare a report for the court
    B. determine whether the charge against the client is valid
    C. assist the client in examining his involvement in the charges against him
    D. assist the attorney in preparing the client for his trial

21. A new client has an argument with the agency receptionist before her initial meeting with the social worker. Upon entering the office, the client says to the social worker, in an angry tone, "Why are you looking at me like that?" This remark is an example of which of the following defense mechanisms?

    A. Displacement
    B. Projection
    C. Reaction formation
    D. Sublimation

22. An adult client, arrested for exposing himself, reports that he was urinating after excessive drinking. This is his third arrest for the same offense. He is depressed, anxious, and markedly distressed by his behavior. This client is **BEST** described by which of the following DSM-IV diagnostic categories?

A. Narcissistic personality disorder
B. Gender identity disorder
C. Exhibitionism
D. Alcohol dependence

23. A woman is referred to a hospital social worker by the emergency room physician, who states that the woman must be admitted to the hospital immediately. The woman tells the social worker that she moved to the community only last month and does not have family or friends who can care for her two preschool children during her hospitalization. The social worker's primary responsibility in this situation is to:

    A. secure emergency financial assistance for the woman so that she can pay for the necessary child care
    B. ask the physician to delay the hospitalization until appropriate child care arrangements are made
    C. find a close relative of the children to care for them as soon as possible
    D. assist the client in arranging a temporary placement for the children

24. A social worker tells his supervisor that he is very uncomfortable and anxious when seeing a client described as "intimidating" and "bullying" to others. The social worker expresses feelings of frustration, saying that nothing he says or does seems to work for the client. Initially, the supervisor's **MOST** helpful approach would be to:

    A. observe the next interview through a two-way mirror
    B. recommend that the next session with the client be taped
    C. role-play the situation with the social worker
    D. suggest appropriate reading materials

25. A manic episode includes all of the following characteristics **EXCEPT**:

    A. distractibility
    B. depersonalization
    C. change in sleep pattern
    D. increased involvement in pleasurable activities

KEY (CORRECT ANSWERS)

1.	B	11.	C
2.	D	12.	C
3.	A	13.	D
4.	D	14.	D
5.	C	15.	A
6.	A	16.	C
7.	C	17.	A
8.	B	18.	D
9.	D	19.	A
10.	A	20.	C

21. B
22. C
23. D
24. C
25. B

TEST 2

DIRECTIONS: Each question or incomplete statement is followed by several suggested answers or completions. Select the one that BEST answers the question or completes the statement. *PRINT THE LETTER OF THE CORRECT ANSWER IN THE SPACE AT THE RIGHT.*

1. The Draw-a-Person test provides diagnostic information about the client's:

    A. personality structure
    B. eye-motor coordination
    C. thought processes
    D. self-image

2. According to psychoanalytic theory, which of the following is associated with the development of neurosis?

    A. Interpersonal struggle
    B. Emotion
    C. Impulsivity
    D. Individuation

3. In working with an African-American family, it is **MOST** important for the social worker to:

    A. acknowledge possible differences in ethnic background early in the relationship
    B. provide directions and instructions to effect a change in the family's negotiation with social institutions
    C. encourage contact with the extended family as a source of material and emotional support
    D. establish contact with members of the family's church to assure them a social support system

4. A social worker has seen a family for four months, with the initial focus on the youngest child's school attendance problems. During the last two months, the child has been absent from school only once. In the last session of the planned termination, the mother reported that she was to be admitted to the hospital for surgery the following week. The social worker's **BEST** course of action is to:

    A. refer the family to a hospital social worker when the mother is admitted
    B. reevaluate with the family the decision to terminate
    C. discontinue treatment, arranging a session when the mother is again able to attend
    D. proceed with plans for the termination of family treatment

5. During an initial session with a social worker, the client describes herself as a very "private person" who doesn't like to talk about herself. She expresses deep concern and anxiety about confidentially and asks the social worker whether "everything I tell you will remain private, and just between us?" The social worker should **FIRST**:

    A. explore the basis of the client's anxiety about confidentiality
    B. discuss the difference between self-disclosure and confidentiality
    C. comment on the client's focus on the confidentiality issue
    D. discuss with the client the limits on confidentiality

6. A social worker in a regional social advocacy organization is requested by citizens in an economically depressed rural area to help improve the area's social and economic condition. Recent growth in a nearby urban area has begun to stir citizens' excitement over new employment opportunities as well as fear over unwanted encroachment. The **MOST** appropriate initial strategy for the social worker to employ with the citizen group is to:

    A. educate group members regarding political strategies for gaining power
    B. assess and document the range of services and needs in the community
    C. orient the citizen group to ways they can collect and analyze community data
    D. facilitate problem-solving and communication skills within the community

7. A couple seeks conjoint therapy from a social worker. After an initial assessment, the social worker's **MOST** appropriate intervention is to:

    A. arrange separate sessions for each client to openly express feelings about the other
    B. foster direct communication with the couple in joint sessions
    C. complete a social and developmental history for each partner
    D. encourage both partners to confront the other with areas of marital dissatisfaction

8. In an initial session, which of the following approaches is **LEAST** effective in reducing a client's hesitation to engage in the social worker-client relationship?

    A. Acknowledging the difficulty the client may have in sharing information
    B. Asking directly whether the client is willing to cooperate
    C. Providing the client with information about the number of sessions, their length, and the costs involved
    D. Developing a written contract with the client based on specific outcomes

9. A 14-year-old who has been in treatment with a social worker for the past year has a history of impulsive acting-out behavior. The adolescent is becoming increasingly depressed and is talking about suicide. The social worker should **FIRST**:

    A. request that the family monitor the client's acting-out behaviors
    B. refer the client to a physician for antidepressant medication
    C. intensify the exploration of origin and nature of the depression
    D. assess the client's potential for self-harm

10. In providing feedback to social workers, the supervisor should include all of the following comments about performance **EXCEPT**:

    A. noting how the social worker's performance mirrors the supervisor's expectation
    B. commending the social worker on a specific action
    C. publicly remarking on the positive performance of a social worker
    D. pointing out inappropriate work performance when it occurs

11. A 16-year-old who has been hospitalized frequently for control of diabetes was referred to the hospital social worker. Information about the youth's family indicates that the father is an alcoholic, and the parents experience a great deal of marital discord, arguing frequently in front of the youth. The social worker should **FIRST**:

    A. work with the family concerning the father's alcoholism
    B. refer the parents for marital therapy
    C. explore the youth's experiences in living with a chronic illness

D. discuss the youth's feelings about separation from the family during hospitalizations

12. During a first interview, a client informs a social worker that she engaged in sexual activity with her previous social worker. The sexual involvement began a year after the client began treatment and ended when she decided to terminate treatment against the social worker's advice. Which of the following actions should the social worker take?

    A. Contact the previous social worker, confronting him with the client's information.
    B. Consult the state social work regulatory law regarding reporting requirements
    C. Investigate whether the client's allegations about the former social worker are true
    D. Take no action since the sexual involvement took place outside the therapy sessions

13. A client with a history of impulsive, aggressive behaviors, has been seeing a social worker for three months. During a session, he becomes angry with the social worker and storms out. He cancels his next appointment and sends a letter demanding that his records be released to him immediately, or he will take legal action. He adds that he is seeing a new therapist and has no plans to return to see the social worker. The social worker believes that releasing the record to the client will cause him serious harm. According to professional ethics, the social worker should **FIRST**:

    A. document in the file both the client's request for the record and the rationale for withholding it
    B. seek legal consultation regarding the threat to sue
    C. send the record to the client as requested
    D. alert the social worker's malpractice carrier that a suit might be filed

14. Viewing an organization as a system, which subsystem encompasses staff development functions?

    A. Support
    B. Operations
    C. Policy
    D. Service

15. A client who has been referred by his physician to a social worker reports that he has come because of "nerves." He says that for the past six months he has been feeling a lot of muscle tension, and is so "keyed up" and "irritable" that he can't concentrate and focus at work. He also has trouble sleeping and can't control his state of worry at home or on the job. According to the DSM-IV, the **MOST** likely diagnosis would be:

    A. Posttraumatic Stress Disorder
    B. Generalized Anxiety Disorder
    C. Dysthymic Disorder
    D. Major Depressive Disorder

16. A social worker observes a parent reaching out to embrace her four-year-old child. When the child approaches, the parent hugs the child, and then with an admonishing tone states, "You should never be so trusting!" In communication theory, this type of interaction observed by the social worker is referred to as:

A. conditional regard
B. double bind
C. emotional blocking
D. cognitive interference

17. A client is seeing a social worker for relationship problems with her boyfriend. She tearfully describes a recent incident in which he was verbally abusive to her. She reports he blames her for his frequent angry outbursts because she does things he considers stupid. Although her friends and family tell her to end the relationship, she says she loves him, but doesn't like the way he treats her. The social worker should **FIRST**:

    A. encourage the client to face the reality of the boyfriend's behavior
    B. explore the client's relationship with family and friends
    C. suggest reading material on abusive relationships
    D. acknowledge the client's ambivalent feelings

18. A woman who recently separated from her husband is seeing a social worker with her children, ages 10 and 16, in family therapy. The initial complaint is that the 10-year-old refuses to attend school. Using a structural family therapy approach, the social worker should **FIRST**:

    A. see the child and mother separately to explore their reactions to the separation
    B. help the mother take charge by encouraging her to insist that the child attend school
    C. arrange for homebound instruction for the child until he returns to school
    D. discuss with the mother her feelings about the recent separation

19. A woman comes to a family agency for help with her marriage. During the first interview with the social worker, she talks rapidly and intensely about her own history of physical illnesses and hospitalizations, her child's problems at school, and her husband's drinking. The **BEST** course of action for the social worker is to:

    A. listen to the client without comment, summarizing at the end of the interview
    B. wait until a pause and ask the client to specify why she came for help
    C. ask the client to elaborate on her husband's drinking and its effect on the family
    D. acknowledge that the client has many troubles and ask which she wants help with

20. In working with reluctant involuntary clients, which of the following areas is the **MOST** important for the social worker to address?

    A. The client's anger at the treatment referral source
    B. The availability of help for the client
    C. The client's ambivalence toward treatment
    D. The social worker's view of the problem for treatment

21. A social work researcher in a mental health clinic wants to measure the effectiveness of group psychotherapy in the social adjustment of recently divorced women. The researcher develops an instrument to measure social adjustment and administers it to 40 divorced women, half of whom are randomly assigned to eight sessions of group psychotherapy. The remaining 20, placed on a waiting list, receive no group psychotherapy. At the end of the eight group sessions the instrument will be re-administered to the 20 group participants and the 20 women on the waiting list. The design being utilized by the researcher is a:

A. static group comparison
B. pretest/posttest control group
C. quasi-experimental
D. one-group pretest/posttest

22. A client has been referred by an Employee Assistance Program (EAP) to a social worker for a maximum of six sessions. The costs for any additional sessions would be the client's responsibility. During the first session, the client describes longstanding personal and relationship problems that she has never resolved, and notes that she is looking forward to finally having the chance to "solve" her problems. Before developing a treatment plan, the social worker should **FIRST**:

    A. support the client's perception that treatment can reduce stress and tension
    B. advocate with the EAP for additional sessions
    C. explore the client's understanding of the referral and the coverage provided
    D. assess the client's capacity and motivation for longterm treatment

23. A cost-benefit analysis in a human service organization is primarily concerned with:

    A. program costs in human and material resources
    B. economic benefits of program goals to the community
    C. the relationship between proposed and actual costs
    D. comparison of alternative means of reaching goals

24. A social worker chairing a task group can **MOST** effectively organize its work by:

    A. rotating the facilitator role among group members
    B. providing relevant written materials to participants prior to the meeting
    C. agreeing to a consensus form of decision-making
    D. specifying the group's objectives

25. In developing a brochure for distribution to prospective clients, a social worker can include all of the following **EXCEPT**:

    A. assurances that treatment will be effective
    B. level of professional credential
    C. highest relevant academic degree
    D. policy on accepting third party payments

KEY (CORRECT ANSWERS)

1.	D	11.	C
2.	A	12.	B
3.	A	13.	A
4.	B	14.	A
5.	D	15.	B
6.	D	16.	B
7.	B	17.	D
8.	B	18.	B
9.	D	19.	D
10.	A	20.	C

21. B
22. C
23. D
24. D
25. A

EXAMINATION SECTION
TEST 1

DIRECTIONS: Each question or incomplete statement is followed by several suggested answers or completions. Select the one that BEST answers the question or completes the statement. *PRINT THE LETTER OF THE CORRECT ANSWER IN THE SPACE AT THE RIGHT.*

1. A breach of ethical conduct may exist when a social worker: 1.____
    A. discusses sports scores with a client during a session
    B. uses the client's first name
    C. exchanges books to be read for pleasure with a client
    D. exchanges social work sessions for babysitting services by the client

2. A seven-year-old child frequently expresses worry about his parents' whereabouts, is afraid of the dark, cries easily, and complains of frequent stomachaches. The child is MOST likely exhibiting: 2.____
    A. symptoms of abuse and neglect
    B. separation anxiety disorder
    C. conduct disorder
    D. panic disorder

3. Using behavior therapy for treatment of depression reflects the view that depression is the result of: 3.____
    A. role confusion
    B. negative cognition
    C. poor interpersonal skills
    D. absence of positive reinforcement

4. A client, referred by his wife, walked into the social worker's office, talking in a loud and threatening manner. He stated that there is no problem except his wife and it is she who should be in therapy. The social worker should FIRST: 4.____
    A. assure the client that he will have the opportunity to discuss his situation
    B. suggest to the client that his behavior indicates that he has a problem
    C. instruct the client to leave the office until he is better composed
    D. ask the client why he believes his wife needs treatment

5. Which of the following characteristics is usually NOT found in families in which incestuous relationships have occurred?   5.____
    A. Enmeshment of family members
    B. Distorted patterns of communication
    C. Symbiotic mother-child relationships
    D. Moralistic attitude toward extramarital affairs

6. Following the resignation of a colleague and the freezing of the colleague's position, social work employees of a non-profit agency confronted the social work administrator. They said they were worried about the financial health of the agency and their job security. In addition they complained about the financial disadvantage they experienced in working for the agency. The administrator agreed to a special meeting designed to address employee issues. When planning how to present budgetary issues in a way that would ensure client care, the administrator should focus on: 6.____

A. acknowledging the legitimacy of employees' concerns
B. explaining the fiscal environment of non-profit organizations
C. charging a committee to develop an alternative budget
D. eliciting input about programs needing priority resource allocation

7. A 28-year-old client with a long-standing history of drug use was referred by a concerned relative to a social worker. In the assessment interview, the client tells the social worker about frequent cocaine use. The social worker should FIRST:

   A. conduct a family interview to gather a comprehensive biopsychosocial history
   B. begin psychotherapy focusing on the reason for drug abuse
   C. refer the client for substance abuse treatment as a prerequisite to individual therapy
   D. evaluate the client's motivation for change

8. A family came to a social worker because of their 11-year-old daughter's behavior in the family. The daughter is an average student and has a group of good friends. Within the family, however, she barely speaks to her parents, refuses to clean her room, and rarely brings her friends home. In describing the daughter's behavior, the parents contradict each other, argue about the severity of the behavior, and disagree on methods of discipline. Using a family therapy approach, the social worker should:

   A. focus on the interpersonal communication within the family
   B. offer the parents the chance to work on the marital relationship
   C. help the daughter to function in the family
   D. involve school personnel with the family to determine the extent of the daughter's behavior

9. A social worker saw an unemployed client whose fee was paid by a concerned family member. As a result of effective treatment, the client resumed employment. Part of the benefit package included HMO coverage for behavioral health care. The client wanted to use this mental health benefit to continue with the social worker, who was already a member of the proper provider panel. To make it possible for the client to use the coverage, the social worker should FIRST:

   A. direct the client to obtain a referral from the primary physician
   B. explain the necessity of formalizing a psychiatric diagnosis
   C. seek pre-authorization for sessions before seeing the client again
   D. inform the client that a case manager controls the number of available sessions

10. A client in her late 20s tells her social worker that she "can't stand" the way she looks, saying that she is overweight and unable to use makeup well, and that she appears sloppy and unkempt, and has little fashion sense. She ends by saying "It's overwhelming to even think about how to change." The social worker should FIRST:

    A. teach the client stress reduction techniques
    B. focus on the clients strengths and skills
    C. establish specific behavioral objectives

D. work with the client to prioritize her concerns

11. The MOST influential factor in determining the probable success of treatment by a social worker whose client is of a different racial background from that of the social worker is the:

    A. social worker's ability to identify with the client
    B. client's transference toward the social worker
    C. social worker's awareness of self
    D. client's ability to communicate openly with the social worker

12. A couple are being seen jointly for problems "with talking to each other." The husband tells the social worker that his wife was sexually abused as a child and he thinks she still has issues with that. The wife confirms the abuse, but denies that it has any relevance to their marital problems, saying she has dealt with the abuse. The husband continues to focus on this topic even after his wife repeatedly asks him to stop. When she yells at him to "just shut up," he does so and turns away from her. She becomes tense and silent. The social worker's MOST appropriate intervention is to:

    A. suggest that the wife and husband be seen individually
    B. suggest they find a topic on which they have less conflict
    C. recommend that they attend a marriage encounter weekend
    D. process with them the observed communication pattern

13. Which of the following statements is true of BOTH supervision and consultation in social work?

    A. The focus is on a continual process of resolving problems identified by the consultant or supervisor.
    B. The level of responsibility of the consultant and supervisor are the same.
    C. The final decision-making authority rests with the consultant or supervisor.
    D. The consultant or the supervisor focus on helping the social worker deal more effectively with problems or tasks.

14. A social worker asks a young child during an assessment interview, "If I asked your parents what they think about you, what would they say?" The social worker is assessing the child's:

    A. dependence on parents
    B. reality testing
    C. conscience
    D. self-concept

15. The use of silence by a social worker during a session with a client who is expressing a high degree of emotion will be MOST effective in:

    A. demonstrating empathy with the client
    B. relieving the client's tension
    C. developing better rapport with the client
    D. assuring the client that the social worker is listening

16. An adolescent boy in a coeducational inpatient group conducted by a social worker is about to be discharged. The treatment staff recommends that the boy be referred to a group home placement rather than returning home to a chaotic family situation. The group members identify with the boy's feelings of wanting to go home and become furious with the staff for its recommendation. In a group session, they become angry and verbally abuse the social worker. The social worker should FIRST:

    A. explain that the reason the boy should go to the group home is due to the family's instability
    B. explore with the group past negative experiences with group homes
    C. explain to the group that some of the material is confidential because it regards the boy's family and it should not be discussed
    D. acknowledge the group's anger and help members identify the underlying issues

17. Family therapy is contraindicated when:

    A. family members are grossly deceitful and destructive to one another
    B. there is evidence of consistent violation of generational boundaries
    C. family myths and secrets appear to be the family style
    D. the identified client is resistant and unmotivated toward change

18. In establishing a therapeutic relationship with an adult client, the social worker should focus attention on the interpersonal process during:

    A. the initial phase of treatment
    B. the establishment of goals
    C. each phase of treatment
    D. the implementation of goals

19. The major difference between process and outcome evaluation in social work practice is:

    A. outcome evaluation is limited to objective measures; process evaluation involves subjective measures
    B. process evaluation focuses on what was done to achieve results; outcome evaluation is focused on the results
    C. outcome evaluation can be conducted only during the termination stage; process evaluation begins with the assessment stage
    D. data for outcome evaluation is secured from the client; the source for process evaluation data is the social worker

20. During a utilization review phone call, a social worker is asked by the managed care representative to provide specific details of the sexual abuse incidents the client experienced. The social worker should:

    A. provide all requested information to the reviewer
    B. refuse to give specific information to protect the client's privacy
    C. review the release of information with the client prior to providing information
    D. review the managed care contract with the supervisor prior to providing information

21. After careful exploration in psychotherapy regarding mounting anxiety and fear of loss of impulse control, a client decided to seek inpatient admission on a voluntary basis. The social worker arranged for a psychiatric evaluation by a provider approved by the client's managed care insurance company. The psychiatrist refused to support admission and prescribed medication, stating the patient could be stabilized and maintained in the community with appropriate therapy. To help the client understand what happened, the social worker should:

    A. validate the client's plan and send the client for a second opinion
    B. explain the requirements of medical necessity and levels of care
    C. explore the possibility of the client paying for inpatient care
    D. mobilize family members to provide the protection needed by the client

22. In working with adult survivors of childhood sexual abuse, the MOST frequently encountered defense mechanism is:

    A. denial
    B. intellectualization
    C. suppression
    D. projection

23. A client is being seen for an initial session by a social worker in private practice. While discussing her history, the client mentions that she has been hospitalized several times for "depression." When the social worker attempts to explore the hospitalizations, the client become tense and guarded, saying it is "old history." She also declares that she won't give permission for those records to be released. The social worker should FIRST:

    A. explore with the client why this topic appears to be upsetting to her
    B. acknowledge the client's right to decide about release of her records
    C. reassure the client that the focus will be on present issues and concerns
    D. assess the client's current level of depression

24. A social worker who tends to be directive and focused on the client's presenting problem is using which of the following therapeutic models?

    A. Object relations
    B. Cognitive behavioral
    C. Psychoanalytic
    D. Existential

25. A hospital social worker is helping a family plan for the home convalescence of a nine-year-old girl injured in an automobile accident. The family reports difficulty with the school district in arranging for a home teacher. When the social worker attempts to contact the administrator responsible for home teacher assignments, the phone calls are not returned. With the child's discharge one week away, the social worker should FIRST:

    A. contact the superintendent of schools about the urgent need for action
    B. request that the primary physician contact the superintendent of schools
    C. send a registered letter to the administrator with the physician's recommendation for a home teacher
    D. arrange follow-up services with the public health nurse who will provide convalescent care

KEY (CORRECT ANSWERS)

1. D
2. B
3. D
4. A
5. C

6. D
7. C
8. A
9. A
10. D

11. C
12. D
13. D
14. D
15. B

16. D
17. A
18. C
19. B
20. C

21. B
22. A
23. B
24. B
25. C

TEST 2

DIRECTIONS: Each question or incomplete statement is followed by several suggested answers or completions. Select the one that BEST answers the question or completes the statement. *PRINT THE LETTER OF THE CORRECT ANSWER IN THE SPACE AT THE RIGHT.*

1. A client whose mother died recently following a long-term illness states to the social worker that he believes that his angry thoughts about his mother caused her death. The client's thoughts are an example of:

    A. delusions
    B. grandiosity
    C. ideas of reference
    D. magical thinking

    1._____

2. Parents of a four-year-old child are referred to a social worker after an examination reveals no physical problem preventing the child from being toilet trained. The parents reveal that the child has not been able to separate from them to attend nursery school, and often sleeps with them even though they have tried to get him to sleep in his own room. During the assessment phase, the social worker's MOST important focus is the:

    A. parents' use of rewards and punishments with the child
    B. early developmental history of each parent
    C. parents' understanding of the child's developmental processes
    D. ways in which the child affects the parents' own relationship

    2._____

3. A 24-year-old woman tells the social worker that she has felt depressed for the past two to three years. She describes herself as feeling sad, with little energy for work or social activities. She also has difficulty making decisions and concentrating on her work, and has a poor appetite. Assessment information does not reveal an apparent reason for the onset of the depressed mood. The client evidences no delusions or hallucinations. According to DSM-IV criteria, the MOST likely diagnosis for the client is:

    A. dysthymic disorder
    B. bipolar disorder, depressed
    C. cyclothymic disorder
    D. major depressive episode, recurrent

    3._____

4. An individual who believes, despite evidence to the contrary, that feelings, thoughts or actions are imposed by an external source, is suffering from:

    A. delirium
    B. delusion
    C. dissociation
    D. dysphoria

    4._____

5. Which of the following medications is used primarily for the treatment of psychosis?

    A. Haloperidol (Haldol)
    B. Alprazolam (Xanax)
    C. Bupropion (Wellbutrin)
    D. Fluoxetine hydrochloride (Prozac)

    5._____

6. A client manifests the characteristics of the early stages of Alzheimer's Disease. To help the client with the changes in her behavior, the MOST appropriate treatment approach for the social worker to use is to focus on:

    A. an understanding of the client's past behavior to enable her to project her future behavior
    B. providing her family members with a support group of other families with similar problems
    C. treatment sessions structured around whatever the client wishes to discuss
    D. observing the progression of the illness and supporting the client in accepting her losses

7. A new client tearfully reports to the social worker that her father, with whom she is very close, is terminally ill. The client's mother, described by her as "very dependent," has already been calling frequently for support and reassurance. The client says "I just don't know how to cope with dad's illness, my mother's demands and my family's needs," and begins to sob. The social worker should FIRST:

    A. acknowledge the client's feelings of being overwhelmed and sad
    B. discuss a referral for hospice care for the father
    C. identify the client's social and family support network
    D. begin exploring ways the client can set limits for her mother

8. A social worker is seeing a lesbian client who is experiencing feelings of frustration, depression, and sadness related to her inability to conceive a child after unsuccessful treatment for infertility problems. She and her partner are considering adoption, but have been rejected by a local agency because of their same gender relationship. The client feels helpless, and does not think she will be successful in fighting the agency bias against same-gender couples. In assisting the client to formulate goals for intervention, the social worker should:

    A. explore the client's motivation to pursue adoption at this time
    B. evaluate where the client is in her coming-out process
    C. help the client to confront the discriminatory policies of the agency
    D. refer the client for medication evaluation for depression

9. A client is complaining about her friend, stating that she is selfish and insensitive. The social worker asks if this is the same friend whom the client had described the week before as caring and a true friend. The client confirms that it is the same person. The social worker comments that this is a complete change in the client's way of thinking. The social worker is using the intervention of:

    A. Interpretation
    B. Reality testing
    C. Confrontation
    D. Clarification

10. Which of the following actions by a social worker is considered unethical?

    A. Receiving a fee for the referral of a client to another practitioner
    B. Informing the client of fees in advance of services
    C. Engaging in private practice while holding an agency employment
    D. Establishing rates for professional services not commensurate with that of other professionals

11. A social worker, many of whose clients are in crisis, carries a heavy and difficult case load. In discussing the cases with the supervisor, the social worker reports that clients "come in with a laundry list of complaints" and efforts to help them resolve their problems result in the social worker feeling angry and frustrated or distant and bored. The social worker is MOST likely dealing with the issue of:

    A. transference
    B. countertransference
    C. job-related stress
    D. depression

12. When authorization for treatment from a managed care company is requested, the PRIMARY determinant for approval is based upon:

    A. treatment goals that are explicit and measurable
    B. a diagnosis covered by the insurance plan
    C. documentation that medical necessity criteria are met
    D. a treatment plan providing the least restrictive level of care

13. After six marital therapy sessions with a social worker, a couple continued their destructive pattern of fighting. During the next session, the couple began yelling at each other in a loud and threatening manner. The social worker stopped them and stated, "Your situation is hopeless; fight as often as you wish." This technique is known as:

    A. encouragement
    B. reframing
    C. prescribing a ritual
    D. paradoxical directive

14. According to ego psychology, projective identification is a concept that describes the process of:

    A. unconsciously perceiving others' behavior as a reflection of one's own attitudes
    B. consciously imitating the characteristics of a significant other
    C. showing another person how to develop a better self-image through modeling
    D. associating characteristics from a significant person in the past with another in the present

15. The executive director in an expanding nonprofit social service agency increasingly involved the Director of Professional Services (DPS) in overall agency planning and decision-making. To participate and still perform DPS functions, this manager delegated some activities to senior professionals. According to principles of delegation, the DPS could shift:

    A. responsibility for task completion
    B. authority to perform tasks
    C. power and influence
    D. responsibility for managerial decisions

16. In interviewing a client, a social worker seeks concreteness from the client for all of the following purposes EXCEPT to:

    A. avoid emotionally charged topics
    B. elicit the client's specific feelings
    C. clarify a client message
    D. focus on the "here and now"

17. In planning to evaluate social work treatment in an agency, the MOST important consideration is:

    A. the amount of clinical staff time the evaluation will require
    B. whether the results of the evaluation can be applied to other services
    C. information the evaluation will yield for treatment decision-making
    D. involvement of clinical staff in the planning of the evaluation strategy

18. A couple in their mid-50s came to a family agency accompanied by their adult daughter who lives in their home. They describe marital difficulties which began after the husband suffered a mild stroke. The wife said that he has frequent outbursts of anger, has lost interest in his personal care, and is fearful of being left alone. The husband stated that his wife is overprotective of him, and described the daughter as "nervous when I try to do anything for myself." Using a structural family therapy approach, the social worker would focus on:

    A. obtaining a complete history of the marital and family relationships
    B. creating a situation in the interview which would place the husband in a dependent role
    C. exploring with all family members their feelings about the effects of the stroke on family relationships
    D. arranging individual treatment sessions for each family member

19. A social worker used three different techniques with a depressed client, introducing each of the treatment techniques in order over a period of time. To compare the effectiveness of each of the techniques in helping the client reach the treatment goal, which of the following designs should the social worker use?

    A. A-B design
    B. Multiple baseline across behaviors design
    C. A-B-A-B design
    D. Within-series design

20. An adult who has come to a hospital emergency room complains of visual hallucinations, confusion, and restlessness. Physical symptoms include chills, dilated pupils, and nausea. When interviewed by the social worker, the client states, "Nothing is wrong; I just need some sleep. Which of the following substances is MOST likely the cause of the client's condition?

    A. Alcohol
    B. Marijuana
    C. Cocaine
    D. Barbiturates

21. After several sessions in individual treatment with a social worker, a married woman client reveals that she has had an ongoing affair during the last five years. She says that she is unhappy in her marriage but wants to remain with her husband until her children are in college. She believes her husband does not suspect her

infidelity but is often upset that she does not spend enough time with him. The BEST plan for the social worker in this situation is to:

- A. focus the treatment on the client's feelings about the situation
- B. schedule sessions with the entire family
- C. see the couple together
- D. refer the husband to another therapist

22. A social worker has been appointed to the board of directors of a family counseling agency. All of the following are appropriate actions for the social worker as a board member EXCEPT:

    - A. determining the performance criteria for the agency director position
    - B. reviewing data about utilization of agency services by clients
    - C. acting as a paid consultant to agency staff who deliver direct services
    - D. serving as chair of a board committee on service delivery

23. For the fifth session with a social worker, a client arrived ten minutes late. Upon entering the social worker's office, the client remained standing and said in an anxious tone, "I know I'm late, but I had other things to do, I just couldn't leave work today." The social worker's BEST response would be to say:

    - A. "You seem to think more of your work than you do of coming here."
    - B. "Maybe we need to explore what it means to you to come here for our sessions."
    - C. "I know that your work is important, but my time is valuable. We will just have less time together today."
    - D. "You seem to think that I would be angry with you for being late today. Let's talk about what you anticipated I would say."

24. When reviewing a social worker's performance, the supervisor recognized that the social worker conveyed little empathy toward clients who had recently left welfare and were holding first jobs. In order to help the social worker increase the number of empathetically accurate statements made to clients, the supervisor should:

    - A. explain welfare-to-work procedures from the client's perspective
    - B. suggest that the social worker enter therapy to become a more empathic person
    - C. model empathic communication when engaging with the worker
    - D. assert clearly the agency's commitment to supporting these clients

25. Borderline personality disorder is characterized by all of the following characteristics EXCEPT:
    - A. intense long-term relationships
    - B. primitive delusional fantasies
    - C. lack of control of aggressive drives
    - D. self-destructive behavior

KEY (CORRECT ANSWERS)

1. D
2. C
3. A
4. B
5. A

6. D
7. A
8. C
9. C
10. A

11. B
12. C
13. D
14. A
15. B

16. A
17. C
18. B
19. D
20. C

21. A
22. C
23. D
24. C
25. A

EXAMINATION SECTION
TEST 1

DIRECTIONS: Each question or incomplete statement is followed by several suggested answers or completions. Select the one that BEST answers the question or completes the statement. *PRINT THE LETTER OF THE CORRECT ANSWER IN THE SPACE AT THE RIGHT.*

1. The culture-of-poverty theories of the late 1960s implied that cultural values concerning the control of sexual activity and the value of marriage were the _____ rather than the _____ of poverty.

    A. best aspects of; worst aspects of
    B. results; causes
    C. causes; results
    D. causes; unintended consequences

    1._____

2. Two kinds of conflicts that underlie much of the controversy and discussion of major public issues concerning the family are

    A. child care and the family wage
    B. women's autonomy and beliefs about *natural* roles
    C. women's autonomy and income assistance to the poor
    D. women's dominance and child care

    2._____

3. Too much emphasis on the *structural causation of* changes in family structures among the poor ignores evidence regarding

    A. proliferation of low wage jobs
    B. increasing male joblessness in the inner city
    C. the benefits of postponing childbearing
    D. racial prejudice

    3._____

4. The proponents of welfare reform argue that work requirements for mothers will have positive consequences. Which of the following is NOT one of positive consequences they predict?

    A. Increased self-esteem will make them better mothers.
    B. Holding a job will help families establish set routines.
    C. Children will benefit from enriched daycare facilities.
    D. Employed mothers will be better role models.

    4._____

5. If current rates of immigration and births were to continue, by the year 2050 the percent of the U.S. population comprised of white Europeans would be approximately _____ percent.

    A. 60   B. 50   C. 35   D. 25

    5._____

6. _____ networks are superior in allowing people to be upwardly mobile.

    A. Marriage-based   B. Female-centered kin
    C. Male-centered kin   D. Cohabitation-based

    6._____

7. Most government involvement in family support is based on a concern about

   A. votes
   B. keeping employees happy and working
   C. dependents, especially children and the elderly
   D. distributing excess monies fairly to all groups

8. Which of the following was NOT one of the changes that contributed to the end of traditional courtship patterns in the United States?

   A. Migration from rural areas to cities
   B. Higher standards of living
   C. Growth in passionate love as a basis for marriage
   D. Extended period of adolescence as a stage of development

9. The longer a woman remains on welfare, the _____ she is to give birth.

   A. more likely
   B. less likely
   C. there is no correlation
   D. none of the above

10. In samples of welfare households, most current household heads grew up in the _____ class.

    A. welfare
    B. middle
    C. working
    D. poor relief

11. The *family duty* blueprint was undermined by

    A. changes in the sexual division of labor
    B. the sexual revolution
    C. the automobile
    D. the emergence of dating among youth

12. Most laboratory studies of married couples as they discussed problems revealed that _____ was a better predictor of a distressed or nondistressed marriage than _____.

    A. verbal behavior; nonverbal behavior
    B. open conflict; nonverbal behavior
    C. nonverbal behavior; verbal behavior
    D. expressed anger; body language

13. Since the 1960s, there has been a shift away from relative care of preschoolers to center care of preschoolers. This is due to

    A. women on welfare relying on state subsidized center care
    B. the increasing proportion of single parents
    C. decreasing labor force participation among women with infants
    D. increased father involvement in childcare

14. According to research on images of romance, romances set in the American West are increasingly about   14.____

    A. resolution of gender disputes through violence
    B. how to resolve male-female conflict over the increasing commitment of women to work
    C. preference for cohabitation over marriage
    D. the declining influence of feminism on American women and their attitudes

15. According to belief on changing images of romance since the 1970s, the overall bestselling genre of popular fiction in the U.S. today is   15.____

    A. science fiction for women   B. time-travel
    C. mystery fiction for women   D. romance

16. An article on the blueprints of love and research on contemporary images of romance both use which of the following research methods?   16.____

    A. Content analysis of popular writings
    B. Surveys of readers
    C. Demographic analysis
    D. All of the above

17. During the Victorian Era, married women's supposed lack of erotic interest in all probability actually gave these women   17.____

    A. some measure of control over pregnancy
    B. control over their husbands
    C. the opportunity to have extramarital affairs
    D. freedom from sexually-transmitted diseases

18. The companionship blueprint for the family is an example of the belief that   18.____

    A. trust, commitment, and permanence are devalued in contemporary society
    B. the 20th century family has increasingly emphasized private over public functions
    C. middle class families are taking on the sexual values of working class families
    D. American attitudes and behavior about divorce are increasingly tolerant

19. An egalitarian division of labor between married partners often collapses with the   19.____

    A. birth of a child   B. wife quitting her job
    C. husband losing his job   D. death of parents

20. The tendency of adults to marry those very similar to themselves in race, education, religion, and other characteristics is referred to as   20.____

    A. the New Home Economics   B. heterogamy
    C. the dating-rating complex   D. none of the above

21. American politicians began to talk specifically about family policy in the   21.____

    A. 1950s   B. mid-1970s   C. mid-1980s   D. 1990s

22. Which of the following has NOT contributed to the increase in single-parent families?   22.____

    A. A cultural shift away from marriage
    B. Scarcity of semi-skilled manufacturing jobs
    C. Income assistance programs
    D. True love as a basis for marriage

23. The independent marriage emphasizes   23.____

    A. rigid gender role typing
    B. affection, friendship, and sexual gratification
    C. authority, duty, and conformity to social norms
    D. self-development and flexible roles

24. American family households most likely to be headed by a married couple are from the   24.____
    _____ racial-ethnic groups.

    A. African-American   B. Asian-American
    C. non-Hispanic white   D. Hispanic

25. The total fertility rate is defined by demographers as the   25.____

    A. proportion of women in a given population able to bear children
    B. proportion of men who father children over a period of 20 years
    C. proportion of men in a given population who are not infertile
    D. average number of children that women would bear over their lifetimes

KEY (CORRECT ANSWERS)

1.	C	11.	A
2.	C	12.	C
3.	C	13.	B
4.	C	14.	B
5.	B	15.	D
6.	A	16.	A
7.	C	17.	A
8.	C	18.	B
9.	B	19.	A
10.	C	20.	D

21. B
22. D
23. D
24. B
25. D

TEST 2

DIRECTIONS: Each question or incomplete statement is followed by several suggested answers or completions. Select the one that BEST answers the question or completes the statement. *PRINT THE LETTER OF THE CORRECT ANSWER IN THE SPACE AT THE RIGHT.*

1. Middle-class Americans in the 1930s and 1940s, despite increased acceptance of pre-marital sex, considered love to be _____ sexual intimacy. 1._____

   A. a barrier to
   B. the result of
   C. the best deterrent of
   D. a necessary condition for

2. _____ percent of young adults in the U.S. eventually marry. 2._____

   A. 45   B. 60   C. 75   D. 90

3. Which of the following responses to partner pregnancy is widely shared among unmarried fathers? 3._____

   A. The fathers strongly condemned abortion.
   B. There was a fairly high probability of marriage before the birth of the child.
   C. Nonmarrying, absent fathers tended to be involved in drugs or crime.
   D. Parents strongly encouraged marriage or co-residence.

4. When cohabitating relationships end, most result in marriage. 4._____

   A. True   B. False

5. The *family cap* is defined as 5._____

   A. limitations on state-supported day care subsidies under the new act
   B. the new work requirement for mothers on welfare
   C. the suggested lifetime limit on welfare benefits
   D. no additional benefits for mothers who give birth while on welfare

6. In the 1970s, the sexual double standard 6._____

   A. disappeared
   B. lingered on
   C. became politically incorrect
   D. increased

7. Contemporary romance novels for women idealize 7._____

   A. family
   B. motherhood
   C. fertility
   D. commitment, trust, and permanence

8. The transitions in marriage forms in the U.S. are consistent with 8._____

   A. a greater emphasis on service to others
   B. a greater emphasis on individualism
   C. a greater threat of economic problems
   D. none of the above

71

9. Parents have _____ choices for arrangements for their infants than for their older pre-schoolers.

   A. fewer
   B. more
   C. better
   D. about the same number of

10. The *earned income credit* is

    A. a program of cash assistance to poor, single-parent families in New York State
    B. the same as the family wage
    C. a new modification of the Aid to Families with Dependent Children program
    D. a refundable tax credit to low-income families with children (where a parent is employed)

11. The income gap between more educated and less educated women in the U.S. is

    A. stabilizing
    B. narrowing
    C. increasing
    D. causing more divorces

12. American states _____ in how they regulate family child care homes.

    A. vary very little
    B. collaborate
    C. vary widely
    D. compete with one another

13. Which of the following is NOT a component of the market model of marriage?

    A. Supply of men and women in a marriage market
    B. Rational choice
    C. Resources of men
    D. Preference

14. When there are alternative job opportunities available to young men other than those related to parents' resources (such as farms, for example), the marriage age of young men tends to

    A. increase
    B. decline
    C. remain unchanged
    D. increase initially then decline

15. Women and men experience romantic love

    A. similarly
    B. differently
    C. at different points in the life span
    D. in inverse life order

16. The typical college woman in the 1940s and 1950s

    A. was having premarital sexual intercourse more frequently than the typical girl in the 1930s
    B. had premarital sexual intercourse at the same rate as the typical college man
    C. tended to have sexual intercourse only when going steady or while engaged
    D. went out only on group dates

17. The _____, as well as subsequent U.S. Supreme Court decisions, banned discrimination against women in hiring and wages.

    A. 1964 Civil Rights Act
    B. 1970 Title XX Amendment
    C. Equal Rights Amendment
    D. 1969 Women's Work Amendment

18.

HOUSEHOLD AND FAMILY CHARACTERISTIC PERCENTAGES BY HOUSEHOLD TYPE

Household characteristics	Household type			
	Female heads	Married heads	Single heads	Elderly heads
Household size				
1	2.6	0.2	79.8	93.8
2	34.9	9.0	7.9	4.8
3	29.8	22.1	3.6	0.7
4	16.3	26.1	2.8	0.5
5	8.1	19.2	2.4	0.0
6 or more	8.4	23.4	3.6	0.2
Average	3.2	4.5	1.5	1.1
Living arrangement				
Home	99.6	99.4	78.1	18.8
Nursing home	0.0	0.2	20.0	81.2
Other	0.4	0.4	2.0	0.0
Marital status				
Never married	39.7	-	73.8	13.8
Married	-	100.0	-	3.9
Separated	27.2	-	8.2	16.6
Divorced	31.4	-	12.1	4.2
Widowed	1.7	-	5.8	61.5
Number of generations in household				
1	3.8	9.6	97.2	98.0
2	94.7	88.8	2.8	1.8
3	1.6	1.6	-	0.2
Number of Children				
0	3.9	11.6	100.0	98.7
1	41.8	23.2	-	1.2
2	29.5	26.9	-	0.0
3	14.2	19.0	-	0.0
4 or more	10.7	19.2	-	0.2
Average	1.9	2.3	-	-
Ages of Children				
Less than 6	40.2	36.3	-	-
6-17	56.3	59.1	-	-
18 or more	3.3	4.6	-	-

The above table presents household and family characteristics of one research sample of welfare households. This table _____ the theory that large, extended families live together on welfare.

    A. does not support   B. supports
    C. does not speak to   D. all of the above

Questions 19-20.

DIRECTIONS: Questions 19 and 20 are to be answered on the basis of the following table.

ESTIMATES OF COHABITATION AND MARRIAGE
BEFORE THE AGE OF 25, BY BIRTH COHORT (%)

Birth Cohort	MALES Cohabit	Marry	FEMALES Cohabit	Marry
2000 - 2004	33	38	37	76
1995 - 1999	29	51	26	67
1990 - 1994	24	55	16	72
1985 - 1989	11	66	7	79
1980 - 1984	8	68	3	82

19. What is the MOST likely reason why more women are married by age 25 than men?

    A. Men avoid marriage.
    B. Men are more likely to cohabit.
    C. Men tend to be older than the women they marry.
    D. Women are more likely to have been married more than once by age 25.

20. Which statement is the BEST description of how marriage and cohabitation experiences have changed over time for men?

    A. Fewer men by age 25 either marry or cohabit.
    B. Cohabitation seems to be *substituting* for early marriage.
    C. More men now postpone sexual relationships.
    D. None of the above

21. Marriages preceded by cohabitation have _____ rate of disruption than marriages not preceded by cohabitation.

    A. a higher
    B. a lower
    C. the same
    D. none of the above (the data are ambiguous)

Questions 22-25.

DIRECTIONS: Questions 22 through 25 are to be answered on the basis of the following table.

INFORMATION ABOUT WOMEN'S MARITAL STATUS, BY BIRTH COHORT AND AGE

Generation	15-19	20-24	Ages 25-29	30-34	35-39
Percent Ever Married*					
Generation X	6	37			
Late baby boomers	10	46	71	84	
Early baby boomers	12	62	83	89	91
World War II	15	69	90	93	95
Parents of baby boomers	16	69	89	94	95
Percent Married and Living With Husband					
Generation X	5	31			
Late baby boomers	9	38	58	67	
Early baby boomers	10	54	69	70	71
World War II	15	62	81	81	78
Parents of baby boomers	15	62	80	84	82
Divorced or Separated Women per 1,000 Married-Spouse Present Women*					
Generation X	-	161			
Late baby boomers	-	158	207	224	
Early baby boomers	-	111	174	229	254
World War II	-	65	86	123	179
Parents of baby boomers	-	81	75	83	98

*These percentages exclude women who were separated because their husbands were in military service.

22. According to this table, which birth cohort had the lowest probability of ever marrying by age 24?

    A. Generation X
    B. Late baby boomers
    C. Early baby boomers
    D. World War II

23. Which of the following birth cohorts had the highest probability of EVER divorcing or separating by age 34?

    A. Late baby boomers
    B. Early baby boomers
    C. World War II
    D. Parents of baby boomers

24. Which of the following cohorts had the highest probability of ever divorcing or separating by age 24?

    A. Generation X
    B. Late baby boomers
    C. Early baby boomers
    D. World War II

25. Based on the table *alone*, which of the following birth cohorts would you predict will have the highest LIFETIME divorce rate?

    A. Generation X
    B. Late baby boomers
    C. Early baby boomers
    D. One cannot tell from the table

KEY (CORRECT ANSWERS)

1.	D	11.	C
2.	D	12.	C
3.	C	13.	B
4.	A	14.	B
5.	D	15.	B
6.	B	16.	C
7.	D	17.	A
8.	B	18.	A
9.	A	19.	B
10.	D	20.	B

21. A
22. D
23. B
24. A
25. A

EXAMINATION SECTION
TEST 1

DIRECTIONS: Each question or incomplete statement is followed by several suggested answers or completions. Select the one that BEST answers the question or completes the statement. *PRINT THE LETTER OF THE CORRECT ANSWER IN THE SPACE AT THE RIGHT.*

1. No-fault divorce is defined as

    A. the right to make important decisions about children
    B. a ruling that a marriage has never been properly formed
    C. coordination of divorced parents in raising children
    D. granting of divorce due to irreconcilable differences

    1.____

2. In the era of restricted divorce, countries with a predominantly _____ religion were more liberal about divorce.

    A. Catholic   B. Muslim   C. Protestant   D. Anglican

    2.____

3. In regard to the family economy and mental health, the fact that women are more exposed to environmental stressors than men has been used to argue that _____ explains the gender gap in psychological distress and depression.

    A. work-family conflict
    B. role participation
    C. psychological compensation
    D. biological predisposition

    3.____

4. Across all types of maltreatment, prevalence rates of child abuse are highest among

    A. middle-class families
    B. low-income families
    C. two-parent families
    D. families with older mothers

    4.____

5. Women are forced to choose between

    A. equality and work
    B. parenting success and equality
    C. parenting success and marriage
    D. equality and marriage

    5.____

6. The TYPICAL waiting period for a divorce in the United States is

    A. one year or less   B. two years
    C. five years   D. three years

    6.____

7. The major cause of elder abuse is

    A. dependency of the elder person
    B. deviance of the abuser
    C. lack of attention to the problem
    D. all of the above

    7.____

8. According to prevalent thought on family roles and psychological distress/depression, the WIDEST *gender gap* in psychological distress levels is between _____ men and women.

   A. never married   B. divorced   C. widowed   D. married

9. The poor's response to marital breakdown has been

   A. annulment through the church
   B. bigamy
   C. separation without legal divorce
   D. to divorce quickly

10. Regarding the long-term impact of divorce on children, the *sleeper effect* is

    A. children of divorce on average finish fewer years of schooling
    B. sons of divorce are less likely to marry
    C. daughters of divorce are less likely to form committed, happy relationships in adulthood
    D. children of divorce are more likely to suffer depression during adulthood

11. Who of the following is MOST likely to commit acts of domestic violence?

    A. Employed men   B. Unemployed men
    C. Men with college degrees   D. Men with graduate degrees

12. Under English law until the late 19th century, at the time of their marriage, husband aad wife became

    A. the equivalent of a legal corporation
    B. two legal partners
    C. one legal person
    D. none of the above

13. A MAJOR negative outcome of divorce on children is

    A. a quarter of mothers practice *diminished parenting*
    B. a number of children are *overburdened* by their parents not being able to function
    C. feelings of abandonment and rejection years later
    D. all of the above

14. _____ likely to take time away from career to invest in family relationships.

    A. Wives are more
    B. Husbands are more
    C. Both wives and husbands are equally
    D. There is no definitive data

15. Men tend toward the _____ ideal in resolving the *second shift,* and women tend toward the _____ ideal.

    A. egalitarian; traditional   B. traditional; egalitarian
    C. traditional; economic   D. economic; sociological

16. Research shows that the average number of hours of housework married women do weekly has _____ since the 1970s.

    A. increased
    B. stayed the same
    C. decreased
    D. varied

17. Many corporations view their workers' families as a

    A. plus
    B. desirable connection to encourage
    C. big problem
    D. source of happiness for their workers

18. The two opposing theoretical perspectives explaining why husbands and wives differ in the amount of money they earn (on average) from jobs are

    A. New Home Economics and demographic change
    B. New Home Economics and the theory of patriarchy
    C. the theory of patriarchy and Marxist feminism
    D. Marxist feminism and demographic change

19. Which is the MOST tolerated form of family violence?

    A. Hitting children
    B. Hitting wives
    C. Hitting husbands
    D. Sexual abuse

20. Which of the following is the BEST description of the *medical model* of domestic violence?
    Domestic violence is seen

    A. as an illness and a source of injuries
    B. in the sense of relations of power and authority between men and women
    C. as a traditional way to preserve the family
    D. as arising from evolutionary processes

21. Parental *buffering* is

    A. parents protecting children from daily stressors
    B. one parent mediating between the children and the other parent
    C. reciprocal give-and-take between parents and children
    D. comforting children who are upset

22. Child maltreatment is _____ among single-parent families.

    A. less prevalent
    B. no more prevalent
    C. more prevalent
    D. there is no conclusive data on this subject

23. The BEST definition of *spillover* is

    A. being involved in more roles increases your psychological distress
    B. being involved in fewer roles increases your psychological distress
    C. stressors from one role have an impact on other aspects of life
    D. rewards from one role in life compensate for stressors in another

24. Men whose wives work generally earn _____ men whose wives do not work.

    A. less than
    B. more than
    C. the same as
    D. sometimes more, sometimes less than

25. _____ was the first jurisdiction anywhere in the Western world to eliminate fault grounds for divorce.

    A. New York   B. England
    C. Calgary (Canada)   D. California

KEY (CORRECT ANSWERS)

1. D
2. C
3. A
4. B
5. D

6. A
7. B
8. D
9. C
10. C

11. B
12. C
13. D
14. A
15. B

16. C
17. C
18. B
19. A
20. A

21. B
22. C
23. C
24. A
25. D

TEST 2

DIRECTIONS: Each question or incomplete statement is followed by several suggested answers or completions. Select the one that BEST answers the question or completes the statement. *PRINT THE LETTER OF THE CORRECT ANSWER IN THE SPACE AT THE RIGHT.*

1. While the affectional bonds are normally very strong between a child and both parents, typically there is more _____ between mothers and children than between fathers and children.

    A. disciplinary strictness
    B. reciprocal give-and-take
    C. play-making
    D. authority

2. In the early 1990's, _____ percent of married women with pre-school-aged children were in the labor force.

    A. 50   B. 30   C. 40   D. 60

3. Reported cases of child abuse/neglect are defined as the total number of

    A. children abused or neglected at least once in a given year
    B. children reported under formal procedures to child protective agencies
    C. reports determined, after investigation, to be child abuse/neglect
    D. all of the above

4. Violence is more prevalent in _____ relationships than _____ relationships.

    A. marital; cohabiting
    B. marital; common law
    C. cohabiting; marital
    D. friendly; close

5. Studies done in the 1950s and 1960s showed that those women who seemed to have the most decision-making power in marriage were

    A. not employed
    B. independently wealthy
    C. employed
    D. none of the above

6. Mandatory reporting laws are a good solution to the problem of elder abuse.

    A. True   B. False

7. On average, husbands who work full-time work _____ wives who work full-time.

    A. fewer hours than
    B. the same hours as
    C. more hours than
    D. none of the above

8. The parental *alliance* involves

    A. agreeing on rules for children
    B. joint decision-making when appropriate
    C. relieving of child care duties
    D. all of the above

9. The *stalled revolution* refers to

    A. too many roles with conflicting demands
    B. family production of food and goods they need to survive
    C. the social system based on the domination of men over women
    D. the lack of adjustment by husbands to their wives' employment

10. Increasing income among poor families would eradicate child maltreatment. 10.____

    A. True   B. False

11. Husbands' greater economic power and authority in the contemporary United States is 11.____
    due in large part to

    A. the husbands' earnings and employment
    B. the tradition of patriarchy in the United States
    C. women's expectations that their husbands should have power
    D. their use of or threat of use of force

12. Divorced fathers _____ tend to be more involved in decisions about their children than 12.____
    divorced fathers

    A. with joint legal custody; without joint legal custody
    B. without joint legal custody; with joint legal custody
    C. without jobs; with jobs
    D. that are remarried; that are unmarried

13. Most companies provide some form of childcare assistance. 13.____

    A. True   B. False

14. Most wives receive alimony as part of their divorce settlement, at least for a limited time. 14.____

    A. True   B. False

15. A substantial proportion of elder abuse is _____ abuse. 15.____

    A. spouse   B. brother to sister
    C. sister to brother   D. cousin

Questions 16-17.

DIRECTIONS: Questions 16 and 17 are to be answered on the basis of the following table.

PROFILE OF TIME ALLOCATION BY LIFE DOMAIN
AND SEX (BASE; MARRIED OR COHABITING ADULTS,
AGE 25-74, IN MACARTHUR NATIONAL STUDY OF MIDLIFE)

	HOME	
	MEN	WOMEN
Domestic chores per week	8.8 hrs	18.9 hrs
(range)	(0-60)	(0-60)
Contact with family not in HH at least once per day	29.4%	40.5%
Give advice /support	58.1 hrs /mo	85.5 hrs/mo
Give hands-on care	23.5%	24.3%
% NONE	25.7 hrs/mo	36.1 hrs/mo
Avg. helping		

16. The table above is consistent with the view that

    A. men are more exposed to stressors than women
    B. women are more exposed to stressors than men
    C. men receive more social support than women
    D. women receive more social support than men

17. The number of hours the average married woman spends on weekly housework has _____ since the 1980's.

    A. stayed the same
    B. increased
    C. decreased
    D. increased greatly

Questions 18-19.

DIRECTIONS: Questions 18 and 19 are to be answered on the basis of the following figure.

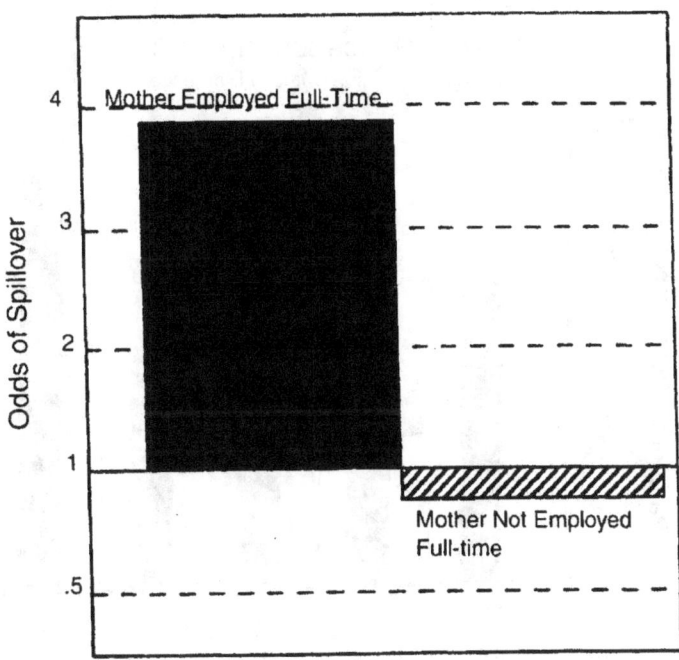

Father's Tension Spillover

18. The above figure shows the odds that a father's argument with someone will spillover (cause an argument later) into the home. The data shown in this figure imply that

    A. women may compensate for home stress by working longer hours
    B. men may compensate for home stress by working longer hours
    C. women experience more role overload than men
    D. men may benefit from being in more traditional marriages

19. The data in the above figure appear to be collected from

    A. the United States Census
    B. a daily stress study
    C. United Nations' studies
    D. school districts

Questions 20-21.

DIRECTIONS: Questions 20 and 21 are to be answered on the basis of the following figure.

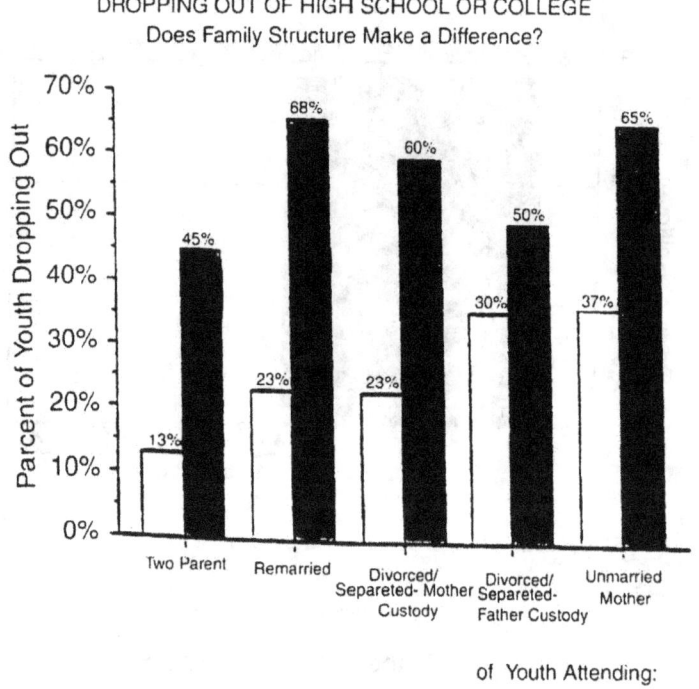

20. The data are from the National Longitudinal Survey of Youth, which oversamples low income families. In this study, the lowest high school dropout rate is for children of which of the following family types? 20.____

    A. Two parent
    B. Remarried parent
    C. Divorced parent, mother custody
    D. Unmarried (single) mother

21. What is the MOST likely reason why the college dropout rate is lower in two parent and divorced father custody families? 21.____

    A. Mothers have less control over children
    B. Fathers tend to have higher income than mothers
    C. Separated parents share equally
    D. Dropouts are unaffected by parental status

Questions 22-23.

DIRECTIONS: Questions 22 and 23 are to be answered on the basis of the following table.

MARRIED MOTHERS' LABOR FORCE ATTACHMENT

	1970	1980	1990
With children under age 18			
Percentage who worked last year	51	63	73
Percentage who worked full-time, year-round	16	23	34
With children under age 6			
Percentage who worked last year	44	58	68
Percentage who worked full-time, year-round	10	18	28
With children aged 6-17			
Percentage who worked last year	58	68	78
Percentage who worked full-time, year-round	23	29	40

22. Of the following groups, which *increased* its year round, full-time employment the MOST from 1970 to 1990? 22.____
    Women with children

    A. under age 18   B. under age 6
    C. age 6-17   D. all of the above

23. Which increased its year-round, full-time employment the LEAST? 23.____
    Women with children

    A. under age 18   B. under age 6
    C. age 6-17   D. all of the above

Questions 24-25.

DIRECTIONS: Questions 24 and 25 are to be answered on the basis of the following tables.

Mean responses to the question: Employed mothers can have just as good a relationship with their children as mothers who are not employed.

Class mean	MEN	WOMEN
	2.39	2.10
25-29	3.07	2.80 (NS)
30-39	3.10	2.47
40-49	3.05	2,20
50-59	3.35	2.60
60+	3.62	2.73

Mean responses to the question: To grow up emotionally healthy, children need to be raised in an intact family with <u>both</u> parents.

Class mean	MEN 2.94	WOMEN 3.54
25-29	2.75	3.19 (NS)
30-39	2.59	3.32
40-49	2.79	3.67
50-59	2.31	3.18
60+	2.15	2.40

1. Response categories: Strongly Agree = 1; Strongly Disagree = 7
2. ALL differences are significant, unless noted otherwise.

The first row presents data from the class survey. Rows 2 through 6 present data from the national survey, grouped by age.

24. Taking both tables together, which statement is the MOST correct summary of the trends?

    A. Middle-aged respondents (early baby boomers) are more socially liberal than current college students.
    B. Women are more socially liberal than men (in general).
    C. Men are more socially liberal than women.
    D. None of the above

25. The pattern of gender and family-related attitudes in this table is most consistent with the issues presented in reading

    A. Mark Rank, FAMILY DYNAMICS
    B. Arlie Hochschild, JOEY'S PROBLEM: EVAN AND NANCY HOLT
    C. Betsy Morris, IS YOUR FAMILY WRECKING YOUR CAREER
    D. none of the above

KEY (CORRECT ANSWERS)

1.	B	11.	A
2.	D	12.	A
3.	B	13.	B
4.	C	14.	B
5.	C	15.	A
6.	B	16.	B
7.	C	17.	C
8.	D	18.	D
9.	D	19.	B
10.	B	20.	A

21. B
22. B
23. C
24. B
25. B

EXAMINATION SECTION
TEST 1

DIRECTIONS: Each question or incomplete statement is followed by several suggested answers or completions. Select the one that BEST answers the question or completes the statement. *PRINT THE LETTER OF IN THE CORRECT ANSWER THE SPACE AT THE RIGHT.*

1. Reports show that more men than women are physically handicapped MAINLY because 1.____

    A. women are instinctively more cautious than men
    B. men are more likely to have congenital deformities
    C. women tend to seek surgical remedies because of greater concern over personal appearance
    D. men have lower ability to recover from injury
    E. men are more likely to be exposed to hazardous conditions

2. Of the following, the explanation married women give MOST frequently for seeking employment outside the home is that they wish to 2.____

    A. escape the drudgeries of home life
    B. develop secondary employment skills
    C. maintain an emotionally satisfying career
    D. provide the main support for the family
    E. supplement the family income

3. Of the following home conditions, the one *most likely* to cause emotional disturbances in children is 3.____

    A. increased birthrate following the war
    B. disrupted family relationships
    C. lower family income than that of neighbors
    D. higher family income than that of neighbors
    E. overcrowded living conditions

4. Casual unemployment, as distinguished from other types of unemployment, is traceable MOST readily to 4.____

    A. a decrease in the demand for labor as a result of scientific progress
    B. more or less haphazard changes in the demand for labor in certain industries
    C. periodic changes in the demand for labor in certain industries
    D. disturbances and disruptions in industry resulting from international trade barriers
    E. increased mobility of the population

5. Labor legislation, although primarily intended for the benefit of the employee, MAY aid the employer by 5.____

    A. increasing his control over the immediate labor market
    B. prohibiting government interference with operating policies
    C. protecting him, through equalization of labor costs, from being undercut by other employers
    D. transferring to the general taxpayer the principal costs of industrial hazards of accident and unemployment
    E. increasing the pensions of civil service employees

6. When employment and unemployment figures both decline, the MOST probable conclusion is that

   A. the population has reached a condition of equilibrium
   B. seasonal employment has ended
   C. the labor force has decreased
   D. payments for unemployment insurance have been increased
   E. industrial progress has reduced working hours

7. An individual with an I.Q. of 100 may be said to have demonstrated _____ intelligence.

   A. superior
   B. absolute
   C. substandard
   D. approximately average
   E. high average

8. While state legislatures differ in many respects, all of them are *most nearly* alike in

   A. provisions for retirement of members
   B. rate of pay
   C. length of legislative sessions
   D. method of selection of their members
   E. length of term of office

9. If a state passed a law in a field under Congressional jurisdiction and if Congress subsequently passed contrary legislation, the state provision would be

   A. regarded as never having existed
   B. valid until the next session of the state legislature, which would be obliged to repeal it
   C. superseded by the federal statute
   D. ratified by Congress
   E. still operative in the state involved

10. Power to pardon offenses committed against the people of the United States is vested in the

    A. Supreme Court of the United States
    B. United States District Courts
    C. Federal Bureau of Investigation
    D. United States Parole Board
    E. President of the United States

11. As distinguished from formal social control of an individual's behavior, an example of informal social control is that exerted by

    A. public opinion
    B. religious doctrine
    C. educational institutions
    D. statutes
    E. public health measures

12. The PRINCIPAL function of the jury in a jury trial is to decide questions of

    A. equity
    B. fact
    C. injunction
    D. contract
    E. law

13. Of the following rights of an individual, the one which usually depends on citizenship as distinguished from those given anyone living under the laws of the United States is the right to

    A. receive public assistance
    B. hold an elective office
    C. petition the government for redress of grievances
    D. receive equal protection of the laws
    E. be accorded a trial by jury

14. If the characteristics of a person were being studied by competent observers, it would be expected that their observations would differ MOST markedly with respect to their evaluation of the person's

    A. intelligence
    B. nutritional condition
    C. temperamental characteristics
    D. weight
    E. height

15. If there are evidences of dietary deficiency in families where cereals make up a major portion of the diet, the *most likely* reason for this deficiency is that

    A. cereals cause absorption of excessive quantities of water
    B. persons who concentrate their diet on cereals do not chew their food properly
    C. carbohydrates are deleterious
    D. other essential food elements are omitted
    E. children eat cereals too rapidly

16. Although malnutrition is generally associated with poverty, dietary studies of population groups in the United States reveal that

    A. malnutrition is most often due to a deficiency of nutrients found chiefly in high-cost foods
    B. there has been overemphasis of the casual relationship between poverty and malnutrition
    C. malnutrition is found among people with sufficient money to be well fed
    D. a majority of the population in all income groups is undernourished
    E. malnutrition is not a factor in the incidence of rickets

17. The organization which has as one of its primary functions the mitigation of suffering caused by famine, fire, floods, and other national calamities is the

    A. National Safety Council
    B. Salvation Army
    C. Public Administration Service
    D. American National Red Cross
    E. American Legion

18. The MAIN difference between public welfare and private social agencies is that in public agencies,

    A. case records are open to the public
    B. the granting of assistance cannot be sufficiently flexible to meet the varying needs of individual recipients
    C. only financial assistance may be provided
    D. all policies and procedures must be based upon statutory authorizations
    E. economical and efficient administration are stressed because their funds are obtained through public taxation

19. A recipient of relief who is in need of the services of an attorney but is unable to pay the customary fees, should *generally* be referred to the

    A. Small Claims Court
    B. Domestic Relations Court
    C. County Lawyers Association
    D. City Law Department
    E. Legal Aid Society

20. An injured workman should file his claim for workmen's compensation with the

    A. State Labor Relations Board
    B. Division of Placement and Unemployment Insurance
    C. State Industrial Commission
    D. Workmen's Compensation Board
    E. State Insurance Board

21. The type of insurance found MOST frequently among families such as those assisted by the Department of Social Services is

    A. accident   B. straight life
    C. endowment   D. industrial
    E. personal liability

22. Of the following items in the standard budget of the Department of Social Services, the one for which actual expenditures would be MOST constant throughout the year is

    A. fuel   B. housing
    C. medical care   D. clothing
    E. household replacements

23. The MOST frequent cause of "broken homes" is attributed to the

    A. temperamental incompatibilities of parents and in-laws
    B. extension of the system of children's courts
    C. psychopathic irresponsibility of the parents
    D. institutionalization of one of the spouses
    E. death of one or both spouses

24. In rearing children, the problems of the widower are usually greater than those of the widow, largely because of the

   A. tendency of widowers to impose excessively rigid moral standards
   B. increased economic hardship
   C. added difficulty of maintaining a desirable home
   D. possibility that a stepmother will be added to the household
   E. prevalent masculine prejudice against pursuits which are inherently feminine

25. Foster-home placement of children is often advocated in preference to institutionalization *primarily* because

   A. the law does not provide for local supervision of children's institutions
   B. institutions furnish a more expensive type of care
   C. the number of institutions is insufficient compared to the number of children needing care
   D. children are not well treated in institutions
   E. foster homes provide a more normal environment for children

KEY (CORRECT ANSWERS)

1. E
2. E
3. B
4. B
5. C

6. C
7. D
8. D
9. C
10. E

11. A
12. B
13. B
14. C
15. D

16. C
17. D
18. D
19. E
20. D

21. D
22. B
23. E
24. C
25. E

TEST 2

DIRECTIONS: Each question or incomplete statement is followed by several suggested answers or completions. Select the one that BEST answers the question or completes the statement. *PRINT THE LETTER OF THE CORRECT ANSWER IN THE SPACE AT THE RIGHT.*

1. Of the following, the category MOST likely to yield the greatest reduction in cost to the taxpayer under improved employment conditions is

    A. home relief, including aid to the homeless
    B. aid to the blind
    C. aid to dependent children
    D. old-age assistance

2. One of the MOST common characteristics of the chronic alcoholic is

    A. low intelligence level
    B. wanderlust
    C. psychosis
    D. egocentricity

3. Of the following factors leading toward the cure of the alcoholic, the MOST important is thought to be

    A. removal of all alcohol from the immediate environment
    B. development of a sense of personal adequacy
    C. social disapproval of drinking
    D. segregation from former companions

4. The Federal Housing Administration is the agency which

    A. insures mortgages made by lending institutions for new construction or remodeling of old construction
    B. provides federal aid for state and local government for slum clearance and housing for very low income families
    C. subsidizes the building industry through direct grants
    D. provides for the construction of low-cost housing projects owned and operated by the federal government

5. In comparing the advantages of foster home over institutional placement, it is generally agreed that institutional care is LEAST advisable for children

    A. who cannot sustain the intimacy of foster family living because of their experiences with their own parents
    B. who are socially well-adjusted or have had considerable experience in living with a family
    C. who have need for special facilities for observation, diagnosis, and treatment
    D. whose natural parents find it difficult to accept the idea of foster home placement because of its close resemblance to adoption

6. The school can play a vital part in detecting the child who displays overt symptomatic behavior indicative of social maladjustment CHIEFLY because the teacher has the opportunity to

   A. assume a pseudo-parental role in regard to discipline and punishment, thereby limiting the extent of the maladjusted child's anti-social behavior
   B. observe how the child relates to the group and what reactions are stimulated in him by his peer relationships
   C. determine whether the adjustment difficulties displayed by the child were brought on by the teacher herself or by the other students
   D. help the child's parents to resolve the difficulties in adjustment which are indicated by the child's reactions to the social pressures exerted by his peers

7. In treating juvenile delinquents, it has been found that there are some who make better social adjustment through group treatment than through an individual casework approach.
   In selecting delinquent boys for group treatment, the one of the following which is the MOST important consideration is that

   A. the boys to be treated in one group be friends or from the same community
   B. only boys who consent to group treatment be included in the group
   C. the ages of the boys included in the group vary as much as possible
   D. only boys who have not reacted to an individual casework approach be included in the group

8. Multi-problem families are generally characterized by various functional indicators.
   Of the following, the family which is *most likely* to be a multi-problem family is one which has

   A. unemployed adult family members
   B. parents with diagnosed character disorders
   C. children and parents with a series of difficulties in the community
   D. poor housekeeping standards

9. Multi-problem families generally have a complex history of intervention by a variety of social agencies.
   Of the following phases involved in planning for their treatment, the one which is MOST important to consider FIRST is the

   A. joint decision to limit any help to be given
   B. analysis of facts and definition of the problems involved
   C. determination of treatment priorities
   D. study of available community resources

10. The development of good public relations in the area for which the supervisor is responsible should be considered by the supervisor as

   A. not his responsibility as he is primarily responsible for his workers' services
   B. dependent upon him as he is in the best position to interpret the department to the community
   C. not important to the adequate functioning of the department
   D. a part of his method of carrying out his job responsibility as what his workers do affects the community

11. Of the following, the LEAST accurate statement concerning the relationship of public and private social agencies is that

   A. both have an important and necessary function to perform
   B. they are not to be considered as competing or rival agencies
   C. they are cooperating agencies
   D. their work is based on fundamentally different social work concepts

12. Of the following, the LEAST accurate statement concerning the worker-client relationship is that the worker should have the ability to

   A. express warmth of feeling in appropriate ways as a basis for a professional relationship which creates confidence
   B. feel appropriately in the relationship without losing the ability to see the situation in the perspective necessary to help the people immersed in it
   C. identify himself with the client so that the worker's personality does not influence the client
   D. use keen observation and perceive what is significant with a new range of appreciation of the meaning of the situation to the client

13. Of the following, the MOST fundamental psychological concept underlying case work in the public assistance field is that

   A. eligibility for public assistance should be reviewed from time to time
   B. workers should be aware of the prevalence of psychological disabilities among members of families on public assistance
   C. workers should realize the necessity of carrying out the policies laid down by the state office in order that state aid may be received
   D. in the process of receiving assistance, recipients should not be deprived of their normal status of self-direction

14. Of the following, the MOST comprehensive as well as the MOST accurate statement concerning the professional attitude of the social worker is that he should

   A. have a real concern for, and an intelligent interest in, the welfare of the client
   B. recognize that the client's feelings rather than the realities of his needs are of major importance to the client
   C. put at the client's service the worker's knowledge and sincere interest in him
   D. use his insight and understanding to make sound decisions about the client

15. The one of the following reasons for refusing a job which is LEAST acceptable, from the viewpoint of maintaining a client's continued rights to unemployment insurance benefits, is that

    A. acceptance of the job would interfere with the client's joining or retaining membership in a labor union
    B. there is a strike, lockout, or other industrial controversy in the establishment where employment is offered
    C. the distance from the place of employment to his home is greater than seems justified to the client
    D. the wages offered are lower than the prevailing wages in that locality

16. Experience pragmatically suggests that dislocation from cultural roots and customs makes for tension, insecurity, and anxiety. This holds for the child as well as the adolescent, for the new immigrant as well as the second-generation citizen.
    Of the following, the MOST important implication of the above statement for a social worker in any setting is that

    A. anxiety, distress, and incapacity are always personal and can be understood best only through an understanding of the child's present cultural environment
    B. in order to resolve the conflicts caused by the displacement of a child from a home with one cultural background to one with another, it is essential that the child fully replace his old culture with the new one
    C. no treatment goal can be envisaged for a dislocated child which does not involve a value judgment which is itself culturally determined
    D. anxiety and distress result from a child's reaction to culturally oriented treatment goals

17. Accepting the fact that mentally gifted children represent superior heredity, the United States faces an important eugenic problem CHIEFLY because

    A. unless these mentally gifted children mature and reproduce more rapidly than the less intelligent children, the nation is heading for a lowering of the average intelligence of its people
    B. although the mentally gifted child always excels scholastically, he generally has less physical stamina than the normal child and tends to lower the nation's population physically
    C. the mentally subnormal are increasing more rapidly than the mentally gifted in America, thus affecting the overall level of achievement of the gifted child
    D. unless the mental level of the general population is raised to that of the gifted child, the mentally gifted will eventually usurp the reigns of government and dominate the mentally weaker

18. The form of psychiatric treatment which requires the LEAST amount of participation on the part of the patient is

    A. psychoanalysis
    B. psychotherapy
    C. shock therapy
    D. non-directive therapy

19. Tests administered by psychologists for the PRIMARY purpose of measuring intelligence are known as _____ tests.

    A. projective
    B. validating
    C. psychometric
    D. apperception

20. In recent years, there have been some significant changes in the treatment of patients in state psychiatric hospitals. These changes are PRIMARILY caused by the use of

    A. electric shock therapy
    B. tranquilizing drugs
    C. steroids
    D. the open-ward policy

21. The psychological test which makes use of a set of twenty pictures, each depicting a dramatic scene, is known as the

    A. Goodenough Test
    B. Thematic Apperception Test
    C. Minnesota Multiphasic Personality Inventory
    D. Healy Picture Completion Test

22. One of the MOST effective ways in which experimental psychologists have been able to study the effects on personality of heredity and environment has been through the study of

    A. primitive cultures
    B. identical twins
    C. mental defectives
    D. newborn infants

23. In hospitals with psychiatric divisions, the psychiatric function is PREDOMINANTLY that of

    A. the training of personnel in all psychiatric disciplines
    B. protection of the community against potentially dangerous psychiatric patients
    C. research and study of psychiatric patients so that new knowledge and information can be made generally available
    D. short-term hospitalization designed to determine diagnosis and recommendations for treatment

24. Predictions of human behavior on the basis of past behavior frequently are INACCURATE because

    A. basic patterns of human behavior are in a continual state of flux
    B. human behavior is not susceptible to explanation of a scientific nature
    C. the underlying psychological mechanisms of behavior are not completely understood
    D. quantitative techniques for the measurement of stimuli and responses are unavailable

25. Socio-cultural factors are being re-evaluated in casework practice as they influence both the worker and the client in their participation in the casework process.
Of the following factors, the one which is currently being studied MOST widely is the

A. social class of worker and client and its significance in casework
B. difference in native intelligence which can be ascribed to racial origin of an individual
C. cultural values affecting the areas in which an individual functions
D. necessity in casework treatment of the client's membership in an organized religious group

25.____

KEY (CORRECT ANSWERS)

1. A
2. D
3. B
4. A
5. B

6. B
7. B
8. C
9. B
10. D

11. D
12. C
13. D
14. C
15. C

16. C
17. A
18. C
19. C
20. B

21. B
22. B
23. D
24. C
25. C

EXAMINATION SECTION
TEST 1

DIRECTIONS: Each question or incomplete statement is followed by several suggested answers or completions. Select the one that BEST answers the question or completes the statement. *PRINT THE LETTER OF THE CORRECT ANSWER IN THE SPACE AT THE RIGHT.*

1. Which of the following provides the BEST rationale for increased government involvement in solving current urban problems? 1.____
   A. The cities are not so badly off as they seem to be.
   B. Additional research and experimentation is needed to develop solutions to urban problems.
   C. Our current urban problems have obvious and simple solutions.
   D. The only thing that prevents us from solving urban problems is public opinion.

2. Ethnic identity as a factor in urban America 2.____
   A. has virtually disappeared with the rapid assimilation of second and third generation immigrants
   B. has little influence on patterns of occupational mobility
   C. has become an increasingly important determinant of residential choices
   D. continues to exercise an influence on voting behavior

3. In recent years, there has been a move to decentralize the governmental structure of some of our largest cities. 3.____
   The one of the following which provides the WEAKEST argument in favor of decentralization is that decentralization will help to
   A. increase administrative responsiveness to neighborhood needs
   B. promote local democracy by developing local leaders
   C. diminish conflict between communities
   D. develop community cohesion

4. The decentralization and diffusion of metropolitan areas has resulted in 4.____
   A. a dramatic decline in the overall population density of the central city
   B. spatial segregation on the basis of race, ethnicity, and class
   C. slow-down in the rate of suburban growth in comparison to central city growth
   D. benefit to persons from lower socio-economic levels by reducing the population density of the poorest sections of the central city

5. The concentration of the poor in the core areas of the modern decentralized metropolis can BEST be explained by the 5.____
   A. failure of public transport systems to follow the new multi-centered pattern of commercial and industrial dispersion
   B. absence of low-skilled jobs in outlying industrial and commercial sub centers

2 (#1)

C. availability of inexpensive goods and services in the central city
D. need such people feel for the security of familiar surroundings

6. Of the following, the MOST serious shortcoming of urban renewal has been that it has
   A. not attempted to modernize aging downtown areas
   B. curtailed industrial and commercial expansion in the cities
   C. failed to provide adequate housing for poor families forced to move out of their old neighborhoods
   D. not stimulated public support for public housing appropriations

6.____

7. The vast majority of blacks who had migrated from the South to northern cities had done so PRIMARILY in order to
   A. join friends and relatives
   B. take specific jobs or look for work
   C. take advantage of superior educational facilities
   D. escape southern racial prejudices

7.____

8. The one of the following that is the CHIEF justification for developing area-wide planning in health care is that such planning is likely to
   A. promote effective use of a community's total health resources
   B. minimize the need for consumer participation
   C. reduce the total cost of medical care in a community
   D. reduce the number of physicians needed in a community

8.____

9. Of the following, the CHIEF reason that the gridiron design, which consists of straight vertical streets that lie perpendicular to horizontal streets, became the dominant planning motif in urban America is that it
   A. facilitated the movement of automobile traffic to central locations
   B. was a convenient and efficient form of subdividing real estate to maximize its utilization
   C. provided fixed boundaries for neighborhoods
   D. could be easily adapted to topographical variations

9.____

10. Which of the following is generally the LARGEST cost factor in acquiring and owning a home?
    A. Building materials   B. Skilled labor
    C. Interest on mortgage   D. Builder's profit

10.____

11. The federally funded job training programs of the 1960's were INITIALLY conceived on the assumption that
    A. the unemployed lacked the necessary skills to qualify for existing job vacancies
    B. people who dropped out of the labor force lost their motivation to work
    C. public assistance made low wage jobs unattractive to the unemployed
    D. the unemployed would not take menial jobs

11.____

12. Which of the following statements about the urban poor is ACCURATE? 12.____
    A. The proportion of poor people in central cities is the same as in suburbs.
    B. Persons under the age of eighteen constitute the largest group of poor persons.
    C. The number of poor persons living in households headed by women has declined.
    D. The majority of poor persons are in households headed by men under the age of sixty-five.

13. Which one of the following statements concerning health care in America is CORRECT? 13.____
    A. All accepted indices indicate that our general health status is higher than that of other countries.
    B. The quality of our doctors and nurses is higher than in other countries.
    C. All people have equal access to the same quality of such care.
    D. The cost of the same quality of care is lower than in most other countries.

14. Of the following, the MOST serious shortcoming of low income public housing sponsored by the federal government is that 14.____
    A. income limitations are imposed upon the tenants
    B. housing administrators place too few restrictions on tenant activities
    C. it competes with the private housing market
    D. it has been built primarily in old and dilapidated neighborhoods

15. Which of the following is the LEAST important factor contributing to the residential segregation of blacks in metropolitan areas? 15.____
    A. Violence against the black renter and homeowner in white neighborhoods
    B. Fear by whites that the economic value of their property will decline if blacks move into white neighborhoods
    C. Personal preferences of blacks and whites
    D. Fear by whites that the quality of schools will decline if blacks move into white neighborhoods

16. Which of the following is the MOST regressive form of local taxation? 16.____
    _____ tax.
    A. General sales   B. Property
    C. Personal income   D. Corporate income

17. The property tax has come under attack in metropolitan regions because 17.____
    A. it fails to discriminate between different types of property within a single taxing jurisdiction
    B. insufficient revenues are raised by the tax
    C. it fails to tax improvements in property
    D. the same type of property is taxed at different rates in different communities within a region

18. Advocates of the culture of poverty hypothesis maintain that remedial action should center on the
    A. discriminatory practices against minorities
    B. lack of work opportunity
    C. attitudes and behavior of the poor
    D. inequitable distribution of educational facilities

19. The one of the following statements concerning crime in our large cities which is LEAST accurate is that
    A. the readily availability of valuable goods in our affluent society has contributed to the increase in crime
    B. young people have a higher crime rate than adults
    C. the increased ability of poor persons to move about the city has contributed to the increase in crime
    D. murder, rape, and aggravated assault constitute the majority of serious crimes as defined by the F.B.I.'s Uniform Crime Reports

20. In assessing the impact of the automobile and public mass transportation on urban population congestion, it is MOST accurate to state that
    A. the construction of an elaborate metropolitan expressway system will relieve such congestion
    B. neither the automobile nor public mass transportation can relieve such congestion
    C. adequate knowledge about the relationship between such congestion and various modes of transportation is still lacking
    D. both the automobile and public mass transportation promote such congestion

21. The Supreme Court, in March 1973, reversed previous lower court decisions which had tried to establish that the financing of education through local property taxes was unconstitutional.
    These lower court decisions were based on the contention that
    A. the property tax was applied inequitably in certain areas
    B. the property tax is not an important source of local revenues
    C. the quality of a child's education was dependent on the wealth of the community
    D. districts with a small tax base would have to add a *value added tax*

22. The percentage of local revenues which is spent on schools is smaller in urban communities than it is in suburban communities PRIMARILY because
    A. the need for quality education is not as well recognized in urban communities
    B. the tax base of urban communities is insufficient
    C. other public services in urban communities absorb a larger proportion of available funds
    D. commercial enterprises do not pay school taxes

23. The one of the following which BEST describes the trend of the drop-out rate in public high schools during the last five years is that this rate
    A. rose sharply
    B. showed little fluctuation throughout the period and ended at the same level this year as it was five years ago
    C. declined sharply
    D. showed considerable fluctuation throughout the period and ended at the same level this year as it was five years ago

24. One of the findings of the Coleman Report, EQUALITY OF EDUCATIONAL OPPORTUNITY, was that the degree to which black students felt they could affect their environment and future is related to their achievement AND to the
    A. quality of the teaching staff
    B. number of college preparatory courses offered at the high school level
    C. condition of physical facilities
    D. proportion of whites in the school

25. The concept of cultural pluralism is MOST actively opposed by
    A. the Amish
    B. supporters of black studies as a discipline
    C. supporters of bilingual education
    D. supporters of parochial schools

23.____
24.____
25.____

KEY (CORRECT ANSWERS)

1.	B		11.	A
2.	D		12.	B
3.	C		13.	B
4.	D		14.	D
5.	A		15.	A
6.	C		16.	A
7.	B		17.	D
8.	A		18.	C
9.	B		19.	D
10.	C		20.	C

21. C
22. C
23. A
24. D
25. A

TEST 2

DIRECTIONS: Each question or incomplete statement is followed by several suggested answers or completions. Select the one that BEST answers the question or completes the statement. *PRINT THE LETTER OF THE CORRECT ANSWER IN THE SPACE AT THE RIGHT.*

1. When police provide patrol services on the basis of workload, a high concentration of patrol officers in minority group neighborhoods often results. The police then are subject to criticism both from minority residents who feel persecuted by the police and from residents of other neighborhoods who feel they are not receiving the same level of police protection.
Which one of the following BEST states both whether or not, under these conditions, patrol distribution should be changed and also the BEST reason therefor?
It should
    A. *not be changed*, because community pressure should not be allowed to influence police decisions
    B. *be changed*, because all neighborhoods in the community are entitled to the same level of police protection
    C. *be changed*, because it is necessary for the police to respond to community pressures in order to improve community relations
    D. *not be changed*, because having police concentration in minority neighborhoods protects the remainder of the community from riot situations
    E. *not be changed*, because to do so would deprive law-abiding minority neighborhood residents of police protection to their need

1._____

2. A certain boy is raised by parents who are concerned with status, social position the *right* occupation, the *right* friends, the *right* neighborhood, etc. Social behavior plays a vital role in their lives, and their outlook with regard to rearing children can best be summed up by *children should be seen and not heard*. Following are four descriptive terms their son might possibly be likely to use if he were asked to describe the *perfect boy*:
    I. Being polite   II. Being a good companion
    III. Being clean   IV. Being fun
Which one of the following choices MOST accurately classifies the above statements into those the boy is MOST likely to use when describing the *perfect boy* and those which he is LEAST likely to use?
He is
    A. most likely to use I and II and least likely to use III and IV
    B. most likely to use I and III and least likely to use II and IV
    C. most likely to use I, II, and III and least likely to use IV
    D. most likely to use II and IV and least likely to use I and III
    E. equally likely to use any of I, II, III, and IV

2._____

3. People adjust to frustrations or conflicts in many different words. One of these ways of adjustment is known as projection.
Which one of the following behaviors is the BEST example of projection?
A person
   A. who is properly arrested for inciting a riot protests against police brutality and violence
   B. stopped for going through a red light claims that he couldn't help it because his brakes wouldn't hold
   C. who is arrested for a crime persistently claims to have forgotten the whole incident that led to his arrest
   D. who is arrested for a crime cries, screams, and stamps his feet on the floor like a child having a temper tantrum
   E. who is stopped for a traffic violation claims that he is a close friend of the mayor in order to escape blame for the violation

4. A certain police officer was patrolling a playground area where adolescent gangs had been causing troubles and holding drinking parties. He approached a teenage boy who was alone and drinking from a large paper cup. He asked the boy what he was drinking, and the boy replied *Coke*. The officer asked the boy for the cup, and the boy refused to give it to him. The officer then explained that he wanted to check the contents, and the boy still refused to give it to him. The officer then demanded the cup, and the boy reluctantly gave it to him. The officer smelled the contents of the cup and determined that it was, in fact, Coke. He then told the boy to move along and emptied the Coke on the ground.
Which one of the following is the MOST serious error, if any, made by the officer in handling this situation?
   A. The officer should not have made any effort to determine what was in the cup.
   B. The officer should not have explained to the boy why he wanted to have the cup.
   C. The officer should have returned the Coke to the boy and allowed the boy to stay where he was.
   D. The officer should have first placed the boy under arrest before taking the cup from him.
   E. None of the above since the officer made no error in handling the situation.

5. Sociological studies have revealed a great deal of information about the behavior and characteristics of homosexuals.
Which one of the following statements about male homosexuals is MOST accurate?
   A. Male homosexual activity is engaged in by less than 10% of the population.
   B. Most male homosexuals would like to be cured if it were possible.
   C. Male homosexuals are more likely than other sex deviates to commit assaults on female children.
   D. Most male homosexuals pose a threat to the morals and safety of a community and should be removed from the streets.

E. Most male homosexuals pose no threat to a community and are content to restrict their activities to people of similar tastes.

6. Which one of the following is the MOST important factor for the police department to consider in building a good public image?
   A. A good working relationship with the news media
   B. An efficient police-community relations program
   C. An efficient system for handling citizen complaints
   D. The proper maintenance of police facilities and equipment
   E. The behavior of individual officers in their contacts with the public

6._____

7. Following are four aspects of Black culture which sociologists and psychologists might possibly consider as health aspects:
   I. Use of hair straighteners
   II. Use of skin bleaches
   III. Use of natural Afro hair styles
   IV. Use of African style of dress
   Which one of the following MOST accurately classifies the above into those that sociologists do consider healthy and those that they do not?
   A. I and III are considered healthy, but II and IV are not
   B. I, III, and IV are considered healthy but II is not
   C. None of I, II, III, and IV is considered healthy
   D. III is considered healthy, but I, II, and IV are not
   E. III and IV are considered healthy, but I and II are not

7._____

8. Which one of the following situations is MOST responsible for making police-community relations more difficult in a densely populated, low income precinct?
   A. The majority of residents in such precincts do not want police on patrol in their communities.
   B. Radio patrol car sectors in such precincts are too small to give patrol officers an understanding of community problems
   C. The higher ratio of arrests per capita in such precincts leads law-abiding residents in such a precinct to feel oppressed by police.
   D. Such precincts tend to have little or no communication among residents so efforts to improve police-community relations must be on an individual level.
   E. This type of precinct has a higher rate of crime and, therefore, law-abiding residents are often bitter because they feel the police give them inferior protection.

8._____

9. Research studies based on having children draw pictures of police officers at work have shown that children of low income minority group parents are more likely to see police as aggressive than children of upper-middle class white parents. One police department had a group of low-income children participate in a 20-minute discussion with a police officer, and then allowed the youngsters a chance to sit in a police car, blow the siren, etc.
   Which one of the following BEST states what effect, if any, this approach MOST likely had on the pictures drawn by the children when they were released two days later?
   A. The children showed almost no hostility toward police.
   B. The children showed significantly less hostility toward police.

9._____

C. The children showed significantly more hostility toward police.
D. There was essentially no change in the attitudes of the children.
E. The children showed a loss of respect for the police, who saw them as weak and permissive

10. Following are three possible complaints against police which might be made frequently by blacks living in cities where riots have taken place:
    I. Lack of adequate channels for complaints against police officers
    II. Failure of police departments to provide adequate protection for Blacks
    III. Discriminatory police employment or promotional practices with regard to Black officers

    Which one of the following choices MOST accurately classifies the above into those which have been frequent complaints and those which have not?
    A. I is a frequent complaint, but II and III are not.
    B. I and II are frequent complaints, but III is not.
    C. I and III are frequent complaints, but II is not.
    D. All of I, II, and III are frequent complaints.
    E. None of I, II, or III is a frequent complaint.

    10.____

11. A career criminal is one who actively engages in crime as his lifework. Which one of the following statements about *career criminals* is MOST accurate?
    A *career criminal*
    A. understands that prison is a normal occupational hazard
    B. is very likely to suffer from deep emotional and psychological problems
    C. has a lower average intelligence than the average for the general public
    D. is just as likely to engage in violence during a crime as any other criminal
    E. is less likely to have begun his crime career as a juvenile when compared to other criminals

    11.____

12. Which one of the following choices BEST describes the tactic of non-violent resistance as used by civil rights groups?
    The
    A. willingness of persons to accept unlawful arrest without resistance
    B. avoiding of prosecution for violations of law by refusing to appear in court when required
    C. teasing and verbal harassment of police officers in order to cause unlawful arrests
    D. intentional violation of a particular law by persons unwilling to accept the penalty for violating that law
    E. intentional violation of a particular law by persons willing to accept the penalty for violating that law

    12.____

13. Which one of the following is the MOST accurate statement about the civil disorders that occurred in the United States in the first nine months of 1967?
    A. Damage caused by riots was much greater than initial estimates indicated.
    B. They intended to be unplanned outbursts, not events planned by militants or agitators.

    13.____

C. The principal targets of attack were homes, schools, and businesses owned by Black merchants.
D. There were very few minor riots; either there were major riots or there were no riots.
E. The majority of persons killed or injured in the disorders were police officers and white civilians.

14. Some managers try to achieve goals by manipulating or deceiving subordinates into doing what the managers want. Such a manager normally is motivated by a desire to control people or by a desire to hide his own inadequacies. Such a manager also wants to hide the reasons for his actions from those he manages. This type of manager is often referred to as a *facade builder*. Which one of the following types of behavior is LEAST characteristic of this type of manager.
He
A. shows concern for other people
B. avoids criticizing other people
C. gives praise and approval easily
D. delegates responsibility for administering punishment
E. avoids getting involved in internal conflicts within the organization

14.____

15. Which one of the following choices states both the MOST PROBABLE effect on crime rate statistics of increased public confidence in police and also the MOST IMPORTANT reason for this effect?
A. The overall statistical crime rate would decrease because people would be less likely to commit crimes.
B. The overall statistical crime rate would increase because people would be more likely to report crimes.
C. The overall statistical crime rate would increase because police would probably be clearing more crimes by arrest.
D. The overall statistical crime rate would decrease because police would be less likely to arrest offender for minor violations.
E. Increased public confidence in police would have no effect on the overall statistical crime rate because this depends on the number of crimes committed, not public attitude toward police.

15.____

16. One of the important tasks of any administrator is the development of a proper filing system for classifying written documents by subject.
Following are three suggested rules for subject cross-referencing which might possibly be considered proper:
I. All filed material should have at least one subject cross-reference.
II. There should be no limit on the number of subject cross-references that may be made for a single record.
III. The original document should be filed under the primary classification subject, with only cross-reference sheets, not considered as records, being filed under the cross-reference subject classifications.

16.____

Which one of the following choices MOST accurately classifies the above into those that are proper rules for cross-referencing and those that are not?
- A. I is a proper rule, but II and III are not.
- B. I and III are proper rules, but II is not.
- C. II and III are proper rules, but I is not
- D. III is a proper rule, but I and II are not.
- E. None of I, II, and III is a proper rule.

17. Wherever gambling, prostitution, and narcotics distribution openly flourish, they are usually accompanied by community charges of *protection* on the part of local police.
Which one of the following BEST states both whether or not such changes have merit and also the BEST reason therefor?
The charges
- A. *do not have, merit* because the nature of these operations makes them very difficult to detect
- B. *have merit*, because such operations cannot long continue openly without some measure of police protection
- C. *have merit*, because offenses of this type are among the easiest to eliminate
- D. *do not have merit*, because the local patrol forces probably do not have responsibility for large-scale vice enforcement
- E. *do not have merit*, because vice flourishes openly only in a community which desires it; therefore, it is the community that is providing the protection

17.____

18. The PRIMARY function of a department of social services is to
- A. refer needy persons to legally responsible relatives for support
- B. enable needy persons to become self-supporting
- C. refer ineligible persons to private agencies
- D. grant aid to needy eligible persons
- E. administer public assistance programs in which the federal and state governments do not participate

18.____

19. A public assistance program objective should be designed to
- A. provide for eligible persons in accordance with their individual requirements and with consideration of the circumstances in which they live
- B. provide for eligible persons at a standard of living equal to that enjoyed while they were self-supporting
- C. make sure that assistance payments from public funds are not too liberal
- D. guard against providing a better living for persons receiving aid than is enjoyed by the most frugal independent families
- E. eliminate the need for private welfare agencies

19.____

20. It is often stated that it would be better to abolish the need for relief rather than to extend the existing public assistance programs.

20.____

This statement suggests that
- A. existing legislation makes it too easy for people to apply for and receive assistance
- B. public assistance should be limited to institutional care for rehabilitative purposes
- C. the support of needy persons should be the responsibility of their own families and relatives rather than that of the government
- D. the existing criteria used to determine *need* for public assistance are too liberal and should be modified to include a *work test*
- E. attempts should be made to eradicate those forces in our social organization which cause poverty

21. The one of the following types of public assistance which is FREQUENTLY described as a *special privilege* is
    - A. veteran assistance
    - B. emergency assistance
    - C. aid to dependent children
    - D. old-age assistance
    - E. vocational rehabilitation of the handicapped

22. The principle of *settlement* holds that each community is responsible for the care of its own members and that communities should not bear the costs of care for needy non-residents.
    This was an intrinsic principle of the
    - A. English Poor Laws
    - B. Home Rule Amendment
    - C. Single Tax Proposal
    - D. National Bankruptcy Regulations
    - E. Proportional Representation Act

23. The FIRST form of state social security legislation developed in the United States was
    - A. health insurance
    - B. unemployment compensation
    - C. workmen's compensation
    - D. old-age insurance
    - E. old-age assistance

24. The plan for establishing a federal government with Cabinet formerly called the Department of Health, Education, and Welfare was
    - A. vetoed by the President after having been passed by Congress
    - B. disapproved by the Senate after having been passed by the House of Representatives
    - C. rejected by both the Senate and the House of Representatives
    - D. enacted into legislation
    - E. determined to be unconstitutional

25. Census Bureau reports show certain definite social trends in our population. One of these trends which was a MAJOR contributing factor in the establishment of the federal old-age insurance system is the
    - A. increased rate of immigration to the United States
    - B. rate at which the number of Americans living to 65 years of age and beyond is increasing

C. increasing amounts spent for categorical relief in the country as a whole
D. decreasing number of legally responsible relatives who have been unable to assist he aged since the depression of 1929
E. number of states which have failed to meet their obligations in the care of the aged

---

KEY (CORRECT ANSWERS)

1.	E		11.	A
2.	B		12.	E
3.	A		13.	B
4.	C		14.	E
5.	E		15.	B
6.	E		16.	C
7.	E		17.	B
8.	E		18.	D
9.	B		19.	A
10.	D		20.	E

21.	A
22.	A
23.	C
24.	D
25.	B

INTERVIEWING
EXAMINATION SECTION
TEST 1

DIRECTIONS: Each question or incomplete statement is followed by several suggested answers or completions. Select the one that BEST answers the question or completes the statement. *PRINT THE LETTER OF THE CORRECT ANSWER IN THE SPACE AT THE RIGHT.*

1. You are conducting an interview with a client who has been having some difficulties with one of her fellow-workers. The client walks on crutches. You tell the client that she probably finds it difficult to get along with her fellow-workers because of this handicap.
   To make such a statement would, *generally,* be

   A. *proper;* people are often prejudiced against persons with physical deformities
   B. *proper;* statements such as this indicate to the client that you are sympathetic toward her
   C. *improper;* this approach would not help the client solve her problem
   D. *improper;* you should have discussed this handicap in relation to the client's continued ability to continue in her job

2. The information which the interviewer plans to secure from an individual with whom he talks is determined MAINLY by the

   A. purpose of the interview and the functions of the agency
   B. state assistance laws and the desires of the individual
   C. privacy they have while talking and the willingness of the individual to give information
   D. emotional feelings of the individual seeking help and the interviewer's reactions to these feelings

3. *Generally,* the MOST effective of the following ways of dealing with a person being interviewed who frequently digresses from the subject under discussion or starts to ramble, is for the interviewer to

   A. tell the person that he, the interviewer, will have to terminate the interview unless the former sticks to the point
   B. increase the tempo of the interview
   C. demonstrate that he is a good listener and allow the person to continue in his own way
   D. inject questions which relate to the purpose of the interview

4. "Being a good listener" is an interviewing technique which, if applied properly, is *desirable* MOSTLY because it

   A. catches the client more easily in misrepresentations and lies
   B. conserves the energies of the interviewer
   C. encourages the client to talk about his personal affairs without restraint
   D. encourages the giving of information which is generally more reliable and complete

5. When questioning applicants for eligibility, it would be BEST to ask questions that are

A. *direct*, so that the applicant will realize that the interviewer knows what he is doing
B. *direct*, so that the information received will be as pertinent as possible
C. *indirect*, so that the applicant will not realize the purpose of the interview
D. *indirect*, so that you can trap the applicant into making admissions that he would not otherwise make

6. The CHIEF reason for conducting an interview with a new applicant in complete privacy is that the

   A. interviewer will be better able to record the facts without any other worker reading his case notes
   B. applicant will be impressed by the business-like atmosphere of the agency
   C. interviewer will be able to devote more time to questioning the applicant without interruption
   D. applicant will be more likely to speak frankly

7. When conducting an interview with a client who is upset because of an increase in rent, it would be BEST for the interviewer to

   A. agree with the client that the agency was wrong in raising his rent, as a basis for further discussion
   B. tell the client that unless he calms down the interview will be ended
   C. prevent the client from becoming emotional
   D. tell the client the reasons for the increase

8. At an interview to determine whether an applicant is eligible, the applicant gives information different from that which he submitted on his application.
   The MOST advisable action to take is to

   A. cross out the old information, enter the new information, and initial the entry
   B. re-enter the old information on the application form and initial the entry
   C. give the applicant another application form, have him fill it out correctly, and resume the interview
   D. give the applicant another application form to fill out, and set a later date for another interview

9. After you have secured, in an interview, all the necessary information from an applicant, he shows no intention of leaving, but starts to tell you a long personal story.
   Of the following, the MOST advisable action for you to take is to

   A. explain to the applicant why personal stories are out of place in a business office
   B. listen carefully to the story for whatever relevant information it may contain
   C. interrupt him tactfully, thank him for the information he has already given, and terminate the interview
   D. inform your supervisor that the time required for this interview will prevent you from completing the interviews scheduled for the day

10. In interviewing, the practice of anticipating an applicant's answers to questions is, *generally*,

    A. *desirable* because it is effective and economical when it is necessary to interview large numbers of applicants
    B. *desirable* because many applicants have language difficulties

C. *undesirable* because it is the inalienable right of every person to answer as he sees fit
D. *undesirable* because applicants may tend to agree with the answer proposed by the interviewer even when the answer is not entirely correct

11. A follow-up interview was arranged for an applicant in order that he might furnish certain requested evidence. At this follow-up interview, the applicant still fails to furnish the necessary evidence.
It would be MOST advisable for you to

    A. advise the applicant that he is now considered ineligible
    B. ask the applicant how soon he can get the necessary evidence and set a date for another interview
    C. question the applicant carefully and thoroughly to determine if he has misrepresented or falsified any information
    D. set a date for another interview and tell the applicant to get the necessary evidence by that time

11._____

12. When an initial interview is being conducted, one way of starting is to explain the purpose of the interview to the applicant.
The practice of starting the interview with such an explanation is, *generally*,

    A. *desirable* because the applicant can then understand why the interview is necessary and what will be accomplished by it
    B. *desirable* because it creates the rapport which is necessary to successful interviewing
    C. *undesirable* because time will be saved by starting off directly with the questions which must be asked
    D. *undesirable* because the interviewer should have the choice of starting an interview in any manner he prefers

12._____

13. Empathy can be defined as the ability of one individual to respond sensitively and imaginatively to another's feelings.
For an interviewer to be empathic during an interview is *usually*

    A. *undesirable*, mainly because an interviewer should never be influenced by the feelings of the one being interviewed
    B. *desirable*, mainly because an interview will not be productive unless the interviewer takes the side of the person interviewed
    C. *undesirable*, mainly because empathy usually leads an interviewer to be biased in favor of the person being interviewed
    D. *desirable*, mainly because this ability allows the interviewer to direct his questions more effectively to the person interviewed

13._____

14. Assume that you must interview several people who know each other.
To gather them all in one group and question them TOGETHER, is, *generally*,

    A. *good practice*, since any inaccurate information offered by one person would be corrected by others in the group
    B. *poor practice*, since people in a group rarely pay adequate attention to questions
    C. *good practice*, since the interviewer will save much time and effort in this way
    D. *poor practice*, since the presence of several people can inhibit an individual from speaking

14._____

15. An effective interviewer should know that the one of the following reasons which LEAST describes why there is a wide range of individual behavior in human relations is that

    A. socio-economic status influences human behavior
    B. physical characteristics do not influence human behavior
    C. education influences human behavior
    D. childhood experience influences human behavior

16. An interviewer encounters an uncooperative interviewee. Of the following, the FIRST thing the interviewer should do in such a situation is to

    A. try various appeals to win the interviewee over to a cooperative attitude
    B. try to ascertain the reason for non-cooperation
    C. promise the interviewee that all data will be kept confidential
    D. alter his interviewing technique with the uncooperative interviewee

17. You discover that an interviewee who was requested to bring with him specific documents for his initial employment interview has forgotten the documents.
    Of the following, the BEST course of action to take is to

    A. give the person a reasonable amount of time to furnish the documents
    B. tell the person you will let him know how much additional time he has
    C. mark the person disqualified for employment; he has failed to provide reasonably requested data on time
    D. mark the person provisionally qualified for employment; upon receipt of the documents he will be permanently qualified

18. In checking interviewees' work experience, you realize that the person whom you are to interview is only marginally fluent in English and has, therefore, requested permission to bring a translator with him.
    Of the following, the BEST course of action is to inform the interviewee that

    A. outside translators may not be used
    B. only city translators may be used
    C. state law requires fluency in English of all civil servants
    D. he may be assisted in the interview by his translator

19. Assume that, during the course of an interview, you are verbally attacked by the person being interviewed.
    Of the following, it would be MOST advisable to

    A. answer back in a matter-of-fact manner
    B. ask the person to apologize and discontinue the interview
    C. ignore the attack but adjourn the interview to another day
    D. use restraint and continue the interview

20. Assume that you find that the person you are interviewing has difficulty finishing his sentences and seems to be groping for words.
    In such a case, the BEST approach for you to take is to

    A. say what you think the person has in mind
    B. proceed patiently without calling attention to the problem
    C. ask the person why he finds it difficult to finish his sentences
    D. interrupt the interview until the person feels more relaxed

21. The one of the following which BEST describes the effect of the *sympathetic approach* in interviewing on the interviewee is that it will 21.____

    A. have no discernible effect on the interviewee
    B. calm the interviewee
    C. lead the interviewee to underemphasize his problems
    D. mislead the interviewee

22. The one of the following characteristics which is a PRIMARY requisite for a successful interview is 22.____

    A. total *curiosity*
    B. total *sympathy*
    C. complete *attention*
    D. complete *dedication*

23. Assume that you have been assigned to conduct a follow-up interview with a primary witness. 23.____
    The one of the following which is MOST important in arranging such an interview is to

    A. keep the witness cooperative
    B. conduct the matter in secret
    C. allow the witness to determine where and when the interview takes place
    D. conduct the interview as soon as possible to insure a strong case

24. By examining a candidate's employment record, an interviewer can determine many things about the candidate. Of the following, the one which is LEAST apparent from an employment record is the candidate's 24.____

    A. character
    B. willingness to work
    C. capacity to get along with co-workers
    D. potential for advancing in civil service

25. Assume that you are conducting an interview in which the person being interviewed is using the interview as a forum for venting his anti-civil service feelings. 25.____
    Of the following, the FIRST thing that you should do is to

    A. agree with the person; perhaps that will shorten the outburst
    B. respectfully disagree with the person; the decorum of the interview has already been disrupted
    C. courteously and objectively direct the interview to the relevant issue
    D. reschedule the interview to another mutually agreeable time

KEY (CORRECT ANSWERS)

1. C
2. A
3. D
4. D
5. B

6. D
7. D
8. A
9. C
10. D

11. B
12. A
13. D
14. D
15. B

16. B
17. A
18. D
19. D
20. B

21. C
22. C
23. A
24. D
25. C

TEST 2

DIRECTIONS: Each question or incomplete statement is followed by several suggested answers or completions. Select the one that BEST answers the question or completes the statement. *PRINT THE LETTER OF THE CORRECT ANSWER IN THE SPACE AT THE RIGHT.*

1. The pattern of an interview is LARGELY set by the 1.____

    A. person being interviewed
    B. person conducting the interview
    C. nature of the interview
    D. policy of the agency employing the interviewer

2. Assume that a person being interviewed, who had been talking freely, suddenly tries to change the subject. 2.____
   To a trained interviewer, this behavior would mean that the person *probably*

    A. knew very little about the subject
    B. realized that he was telling too much
    C. decided that his privacy was being violated
    D. realized that he was becoming confused

3. Assume that you receive a telephone call from an unknown individual requesting information about a person you are currently interviewing. 3.____
   In such a situation, the BEST course of action for you to take is to

    A. give him the information over the telephone
    B. tell him to write to your department for the information
    C. send him the information, retaining a copy for your files
    D. tell him to call back, giving you additional time to check into the matter

4. In an interview, assuming that the interviewer was using a *non-directive approach* in this interview, of the following, the interviewer's most effective response would be: 4.____

    A. "You know, you are building a bad record of tardiness."
    B. "Can you tell me more about this situation?"
    C. "What kind of person is your superior?"
    D. "Do you think you are acting fairly towards the agency by being late so often?"

5. In an interview, assuming that the interviewer was using a *directed approach* in this interview, of the following, the interviewer's response should be: 5.____

    A. "That doesn't seem like much of an excuse to me."
    B. "What do you mean by saying that you've lost interest?"
    C. "What problems are there with the supervision you are getting?"
    D. "How do you think your tardiness looks in your personnel record?"

Questions 6-8.

DIRECTIONS: Answer Questions 6 through 8 only on the basis of information given in the passage below.

A personnel interviewer, selecting job applicants, may find that he reacts badly to some people even on first contact. This reaction cannot usually be explained by things that the interviewee has done or said. Most of us have had the experience of liking or disliking, of feeling comfortable or uncomfortable with people on first acquaintance, long before we have had a chance to make a conscious, rational decision about them. Often, too, our liking or disliking is transmitted to the other person by subtle processes such as gestures, posture, voice intonations, or choice of words. The point to be kept in mind in this: the relations between people are complex and occur at several levels, from the conscious to the unconscious. This is true whether the relationship is brief or long, formal or informal.

Some of the major dynamics of personality which operate on the unconscious level are projection, sublimation, rationalization, and repression. Encountering these for the first time, one is apt to think of them as representing pathological states. In the extreme, they undoubtedly are, but they exist so universally that we must consider them also to be parts of normal personality.

Without necessarily subscribing to any of the numerous theories of personality, it is possible to describe personality in terms of certain important aspects or elements. We are all aware of ourselves as thinking organisms.

This aspect of personality, the conscious part, is important for understanding human behavior, but it is not enough. Many find it hard to accept the notion that each person also has an unconscious. The existence of the unconscious is no longer a matter of debate. It is not possible to estimate at all precisely what proportion of our total psychological life is conscious, what proportion unconscious. Everyone who has studied the problem, however, agrees that consciousness is the smaller part of personality. Most of what we are and do is a result of unconscious processes. To ignore this is to risk mistakes.

6. The passage above suggests that an interviewer can be MOST effective if he

    A. learns how to determine other peoples' unconscious motivations
    B. learns how to repress his own unconsciously motivated mannerisms and behavior
    C. can keep others from feeling that he either likes or dislikes them
    D. gains an understanding of how the unconscious operates in himself and in others

7. It may be inferred from the passage above that the "subtle processes, such as gestures, posture, voice intonation, or choice of words," referred to in the first paragraph, are, *usually*,

    A. in the complete control of an expert interviewer
    B. the determining factors in the friendships a person establishes
    C. controlled by a person's unconscious
    D. not capable of being consciously controlled

8. The passage above implies that various different personality theories are, *usually*,

    A. so numerous and different as to be valueless to an interviewer
    B. in basic agreement about the importance of the unconscious
    C. understood by the interviewer who strives to be effective
    D. in agreement that personality factors such as projection and repression are pathological

Questions 9-10.

DIRECTIONS: Answer Questions 9 and 10 ONLY on the basis of information given in the passage below.

Since we generally assure informants that what they say is confidential, we are not free to tell one informant what the other has told us. Even if the informant says, "I don't care who knows it; tell anybody you want to," we find it wise to treat the interview as confidential. An interviewer who relates to some informants what other informants have told him is likely to stir up anxiety and suspicion. Of course, the interviewer may be able to tell an informant what he has heard without revealing the source of his information. This may be perfectly appropriate where a story has wide currency so that an informant cannot infer the source of the information. But if an event is not widely known, the mere mention of it may reveal to one informant what another informant has said about the situation. How can the data be cross-checked in these circumstances?

9. The passage above implies that the anxiety and suspicion an interviewer may arouse by telling what has been learned in other interviews is due to the   9.____

   A. lack of trust the person interviewed may have in the interviewer's honesty
   B. troublesome nature of the material which the interviewer has learned in other interviews
   C. fact that the person interviewed may not believe that permission was given to repeat the information
   D. fear of the person interviewed that what he is telling the interviewer will be repeated

10. The paragraph above is *most likely* part of a longer passage dealing with   10.____

    A. ways to verify data gathered in interviews
    B. the various anxieties a person being interviewed may feel
    C. the notion that people sometimes say things they do not mean
    D. ways an interviewer can avoid seeming suspicious

Questions 11-12.

DIRECTIONS: Answer Questions 11 and 12 ONLY on the basis of information given below.

The ability to interview rests not only on any single trait, but on a vast complex of them. Habits, skills, techniques, and attitudes are all involved. Competence in interviewing is acquired only after careful and diligent study, prolonged practice (preferably under supervision), and a good bit of trial and error; for interviewing is not an exact science, it is an art. Like many other arts, however, it can and must draw on science in several of its aspects.

There is always a place for individual initiative, for imaginative innovations, and for new combinations of old approaches. The skilled interviewer cannot be bound by a set of rules. Likewise, there is not a set of rules which can guarantee to the novice that his interviewing will be successful. There are, however, some accepted, general guide-posts which may help the beginner to avoid mistakes, learn how to conserve his efforts, and establish effective working relationships with interviewees; to accomplish, in short, what he set out to do.

11. According to the passage above, rules and standard techniques for interviewing are   11.____

A. helpful for the beginner, but useless for the experienced, innovative interviewer
B. destructive of the innovation and initiative needed for a good interviewer
C. useful for even the experienced interviewer, who may, however, sometimes go beyond them
D. the means by which nearly anybody can become an effective interviewer

12. According to the passage above, the one of the following which is a prerequisite to competent interviewing is

    A. avoiding mistakes
    B. study and practice
    C. imaginative innovation
    D. natural aptitude

Questions 13-16.

DIRECTIONS: Answer Questions 13 through 16 SOLELY on the basis of information given in the following paragraph.

The question of what material is relevant is not as simple as it might seem. Frequently material which seems irrelevant to the inexperienced has, because of the common tendency to disguise and distort and misplace one's feelings, considerable significance. It may be necessary to let the client "ramble on" for a while in order to clear the decks, as it were, so that he may get down to things that really are on his mind. On the other hand, with an already disturbed person, it may be important for the interviewer to know when to discourage further elaboration of upsetting material. This is especially the case where the worker would be unable to do anything about it. An inexperienced interviewer might, for instance, be intrigued with the bizarre elaboration of material that the psychotic produces, but further elaboration of this might encourage the client in his instability. A too random discussion may indicate that the interviewee is not certain in what areas the interviewer is prepared to help him, and he may be seeking some direction. Or again, satisfying though it may be for the interviewer to have the interviewee tell him intimate details, such revelations sometimes need to be checked or encouraged only in small doses. An interviewee who has "talked too much" often reveals subsequent anxiety. This is illustrated by the fact that? frequently after a "confessional" interview ,the interviewee surprises the interviewer by being withdrawn, inarticulate, or hostile, or by breaking the next appointment.

13. Sometimes a client may reveal certain personal information to an interviewer and subsequently, may feel anxious about this revelation.
    If, during an interview, a client begins to discuss very personal matters, it would be BEST to

    A. tell the client, in no uncertain terms, that you're not interested in personal details
    B. ignore the client at this point
    C. encourage the client to elaborate further on the details
    D. inform the client that the information seems to be very personal

14. Clients with severe psychological disturbances pose an especially difficult problem for the inexperienced interviewer.
The difficulty lies in the possibility of the client's

   A. becoming physically violent and harming the interviewer
   B. "rambling on" for a while
   C. revealing irrelevant details which may be followed by cancelled appointments
   D. reverting to an unstable state as a result of interview material

14.____

15. An interviewer should be constantly alert to the possibility of obtaining clues from the client as to problem areas.
According to the above passage, a client who discusses topics at random may be

   A. unsure of what problems the interviewer can provide help
   B. reluctant to discuss intimate details
   C. trying to impress the interviewer with his knowledge
   D. deciding what relevant material to elaborate on

15.____

16. The evaluation of a client's responses may reveal substantial information that may aid the interviewer in assessing the problem areas that are of concern to the client. Responses that seemed irrelevant at the time of the interview may be of significance because

   A. considerable significance is attached to all irrelevant material
   B. emotional feelings are frequently masked
   C. an initial "rambling on" is often a prelude to what -is actually bothering the client
   D. disturbed clients often reveal subsequent anxiety

16.____

Questions 17-19.

DIRECTIONS: Answer Questions 17 through 19 SOLELY on the basis of the following paragraph.

    The physical setting of the interview may determine its entire potentiality. Some degree of privacy and a comfortable relaxed atmosphere are important. The interviewee is not encouraged to give much more than his name and address if the interviewer seems busy with other things, if people are rushing about, if there are distracting noises. He has a right to feel that, whether the interview lasts five minutes or an hour, he has, for that time, the undivided attention of the interviewer. Interruptions, telephone calls, and so on, should be reduced to a minimum. If the interviewee has waited in a crowded room for what seems to him an interminably long period, he is naturally in no mood to sit down and discuss what is on his mind. Indeed, by that time the primary thing on his mind may be his irritation at being kept waiting, and he frequently feels it would be impolite to express this. If a wait or interruptions have been unavoidable, it is always helpful to give the client some recognition that these are disturbing and that he can naturally understand that they make it more difficult for him to proceed. At the same time if he protests that they have not troubled him, the interviewer can best accept his statements at their face value, as further insistence that they must have been disturbing may be interpreted by him as accusing, and he may conclude that the interviewer has been personally hurt by his irritation.

17. Distraction during an interview may tend to limit the client's responses.
    In a case where an interruption has occurred, it would be BEST for the interviewer to

    A. terminate this interview and have it rescheduled for another time period
    B. ignore the interruption since it is not continuous
    C. express his understanding that the distraction can cause the client to feel disturbed
    D. accept the client's protests that he has been troubled by the interruption

18. To maximize the rapport that can be established with the client, an appropriate physical setting is necessary. At the very least, some privacy would be necessary.
    In addition, the interviewer should

    A. always appear to be busy in order to impress the client
    B. focus his attention only on the client
    C. accept all the client's statements as being valid
    D. stress the importance of the interview to the client

19. Clients who have been waiting quite some time for their interview may, justifiably, become upset. However, a client *may initially* attempt to mask these feelings because he may

    A. personally hurt the interviewer
    B. want to be civil
    C. feel that the wait was unavoidable
    D. fear the consequences of his statement

20. You have been assigned to interview W, a witness, concerning a minor automobile accident. Although you have made no breach of the basic rules of contact and approach, you, nevertheless, recognize that you and W have a personality clash and that a natural animosity has resulted.
    Of the following, you MOST appropriately should

    A. discuss the personality problem with W and attempt to resolve the difference
    B. stop the interview on some pretext and leave in a calm and pleasant manner, allowing an associate to continue the interview
    C. ignore the personality problem and continue as though nothing had happened
    D. change the subject matter being discussed since the facts sought may be the source of the animosity

21. Assume that you desire to interview W, a reluctant witness to an event that took place several weeks previously. Assume further that the interview can take place at a location to be designated by the interviewer.
    Of the following, the place of interview should *preferably* be the

    A. office of the interviewer
    B. home of W
    C. office of W
    D. scene where the event took place

22. Assume that you are interviewing W, a witness. During the interview it becomes apparent that W's statements are inaccurate and at variance with the facts previously established.
    In these circumstances, it would be BEST for you to

    A. tell W that his statements are inaccurate and point out how they conflict with previously established facts

B. reword your questions and ask additional questions about the facts being discussed
C. warn W that he may be required to testify under oath at a later date
D. ignore W's statements if you have other information that support the facts

23. Assume that W, a witness being interviewed by you, shows a tendency to ramble. His answers to your questions are lengthy and not responsive.
In this situation, the BEST action for you to take is to

   A. permit W to continue because at some point he will tell you the information sought
   B. tell W that he is rambling and unresponsive and that more will be accomplished if he is brief and to the point
   C. control the interview so that complete and accurate information is obtained
   D. patiently listen to W since rambling is W's style and it cannot be changed

24. Assume that you are interviewing a client. Of the following, the BEST procedure for you to follow in regard to the use of your notebook is to

   A. take out your notebook at the start of the interview and immediately begin taking notes
   B. memorize the important facts related during the interview and enter them after the interview has been completed
   C. advise the client that all his answers are being taken down to insure that he will tell the truth
   D. establish rapport with the client and ask permission to jot down various data in your notebook

25. In order to conduct an effective interview, an interviewer's attention must continuously be directed in two ways, toward himself as well as toward the interviewee. Of the following, the PRIMARY danger in this division of attention is that the

   A. interviewer's behavior may become less natural and thus alienate the interviewee
   B. interviewee's span of attention will be shortened
   C. interviewer's response may be interpreted by the interviewee as being antagonistic
   D. interviewee's more or less concealed prejudices will come to the surface

KEY (CORRECT ANSWERS)

1.	B	11.	C
2.	B	12.	B
3.	B	13.	D
4.	B	14.	D
5.	C	15.	A
6.	D	16.	B
7.	C	17.	C
8.	B	18.	B
9.	D	19.	B
10.	A	20.	B

21. A
22. B
23. C
24. D
25. A

READING COMPREHENSION
UNDERSTANDING AND INTERPRETING WRITTEN MATERIAL

EXAMINATION SECTION
TEST 1

DIRECTIONS: Each question or incomplete statement is followed by several suggested answers or completions. Select the one that BEST answers the question or completes the statement. *PRINT THE LETTER OF THE CORRECT ANSWER IN THE SPACE AT THE RIGHT.*

Questions 1-2.

DIRECTIONS: Questions 1 and 2 are to be answered SOLELY on the basis of the following passage.

    The new suburbia that is currently being built does not look much different from the old; there has, however, been an increase in the class and race polarization that has been developing between the suburbs and the cities for several generations now. The suburbs have become the home for an ever larger proportion of working-class, middle-class, and upper-class whites; the cities, for an even larger proportion of poor and non-white people. A great number of cities are 30 to 50 percent non-white in population, with more and larger ghettos than cities have ever had. Now, there is greater urban poverty on the one hand, and stronger suburban opposition to open housing and related policies to solve the cities' problems on the other hand. The urban crisis will worsen; and although there is no shortage of rational solutions, nothing much will be done about the crisis unless white America permits a radical change of public policy and undergoes a miraculous change of attitude towards its cities and their populations.

1. Which of the following statements is IMPLIED by the above passage?

    A. The percentage of non-whites in the suburbs is increasing.
    B. The policies of suburbanites have contributed to the seriousness of the urban crisis.
    C. The problems of the cities defy rational solutions.
    D. There has been a radical change in the appearance of both suburbia and the cities in the past few years.

2. Of the following, the title which BEST describes the passage's main theme is:

    A. THE NEW SUBURBIA
    B. URBAN POVERTY
    C. URBAN-SUBURBAN POLARIZATION
    D. WHY AMERICANS WANT TO LIVE IN THE SUBURBS

Questions 3-4.

DIRECTIONS: Questions 3 and 4 are to be answered selecting the BEST interpretation of the following paragraph.

One of the most familiar *type* dichotomies is Jung's introvert versus extrovert. Introverts are motivated by principles, extroverts by expediency; introverts are thinkers, extroverts are doers; and so on. Analysis of the way people react to principle versus expediency situations, however, has demonstrated that most people would have to be described as ambiverts (i.e., they exhibit both introverted and extroverted behavior depending upon the specific situation). Of course, some people behave in a more introverted way than others. A graphic representation of the number of persons exhibiting various degrees of such behavior along a continuum would approximate the familiar bell-shaped curve.

3.   A. Extreme extroverts exhibit deviant behavior.   3.____
     B. The bell-shaped curve would indicate that there are slightly more introverts than extroverts.
     C. A continuum is used to determine whether a person is an introvert or an extrovert.
     D. There is really very little difference between an introvert, an extrovert, or an ambivert.

4.   A. Extroverts are not thinkers, and introverts are not doers.   4.____
     B. Ambiverts *think* more than they *do*.
     C. Ambiverts outnumber introverts in the general society.
     D. Extroverts possess fewer principles than introverts.

5. The fundamental desires for food, shelter, family, and approval, and their accompanying instinctive forms of behavior, are among the most important forces in human life because they are essential to and directly connected with the preservation and the welfare of the individual as well as of the race.   5.____
According to this statement,

     A. as long as human beings are permitted to act instinctively, they will act wisely
     B. the instinct for self-preservation makes the individual consider his own welfare rather than that of others
     C. racial and individual welfare depend upon the fundamental desires
     D. the preservation of the race demands that instinctive behavior be modified

6. The growth of our cities, the increasing tendency to move from one part of the country to another, the existence of people of different cultures in the neighborhood, have together made it more and more difficult to secure group recreation as part of informal family and neighborhood life.   6.____
According to this statement,

     A. the breaking up of family and neighborhood ties discourages new family and neighborhood group recreation
     B. neighborhood recreation no longer forms a significant part of the larger community
     C. the growth of cities crowds out the development of all recreational activities
     D. the non-English-speaking people do not accept new activities easily

7. Sublimation consists in directing some inner urge, arising from a lower psychological level into some channel of interest on a higher psychological level. Pugnaciousness, for example, is directed into some athletic activity involving combat, such as football or boxing, where rules of fair play and the ethics of the game lift the destructive urge for combat into a constructive experience and offer opportunities for the development of character and personality.   7.____

According to this statement,

A. the manner of self-expression may be directed into constructive activities
B. athletic activities such as football and boxing are destructive of character
C. all conscious behavior on high psychological levels indicates the process of sublimation
D. the rules of fair play are inconsistent with pugnaciousness

Questions 8-9.

DIRECTIONS: Questions 8 and 9 are to be answered on the basis of the following passage.

Just why some individuals choose one way of adjusting to their difficulties and others choose other ways is not known. Yet what an individual does when he is thwarted remains a reasonably good key to the understanding of his personality. If his responses to thwart-ings are emotional explosions and irrational excuses, he is tending to live in an unreal world. He may need help to regain the world of reality, the cause-and-effect world recognized by generations of thinkers and scientists. Perhaps he needs encouragement to redouble his efforts. Perhaps, on the other hand, he is striving for the impossible and needs to substitute a worthwhile activity within the range of his abilities. It is the part of wisdom to learn the nature of the world and of oneself in relation to it and to meet each situation as intelligently and as adequately as one can.

8. The title that BEST expresses the idea of this paragraph is

   A. ADJUSTING TO LIFE
   B. ESCAPE FROM REALITY
   C. THE IMPORTANCE OF PERSONALITY
   D. EMOTIONAL CONTROL

9. The writer argues that all should

   A. substitute new activities for old
   B. redouble their efforts
   C. analyze their relation to the world
   D. seek encouragement from others

Questions 10-15.

DIRECTIONS: Questions 10 through 15 are to be answered SOLELY on the basis of the information given in the paragraph below.

The use of role-playing as a training technique was developed during the past decade by social scientists, particularly psychologists, who have been active in training experiments. Originally, this technique was applied by clinical psychologists who discovered that a patient appears to gain understanding of an emotionally disturbing situation when encouraged to act out roles in that situation. As applied in government and business organizations, the purpose of role-playing is to aid employees to understand certain work problems involving interpersonal relations and to enable observers to evaluate various reactions to them. Thus, for example, on the problem of handling grievances, two individuals from the group might be selected to act out extemporaneously the parts of subordinate and supervisor. When this situation is enacted by various pairs among the class and the techniques and results are discussed, the members of the group are presumed to reach conclusions about the most effective means of handling similar situations. Often the use of role reversal, where participants take parts different from their actual work roles, assists individuals to gain more insight into other people's problems and viewpoints. Although role-playing can be a rewarding training device, the trainer must be aware of his responsibilities. If this technique is to be successful, thorough briefing of both actors and observers as to the situation in question, the participants' roles, and what to look for, is essential.

10. The role-playing technique was FIRST used for the purpose of

    A. measuring the effectiveness of training programs
    B. training supervisors in business organizations
    C. treating emotionally disturbed patients
    D. handling employee grievances

11. When role-playing is used in private business as a training device, the CHIEF aim is to

    A. develop better relations between supervisor and subordinate in the handling of grievances
    B. come up with a solution to a specific problem that has arisen
    C. determine the training needs of the group
    D. increase employee understanding of the human relation factors in work situations

12. From the above passage, it is MOST reasonable to conclude that when role-playing is used, it is preferable to have the roles acted out by

    A. only one set of actors
    B. no more than two sets of actors
    C. several different sets of actors
    D. the trainer or trainers of the group

13. Based on the above passage, a trainer using the technique of role reversal in a problem of first-line supervision should assign a senior enforcement agent to play the part of a(n)

    A. enforcement agent
    B. senior enforcement agent
    C. principal enforcement agent
    D. angry citizen

14. It can be inferred from the above passage that a *limitation* of role-play as a training method is that

    A. many work situations do not lend themselves to role-play
    B. employees are not experienced enough as actors to play the roles realistically
    C. only trainers who have psychological training can use it successfully
    D. participants who are observing and not acting do not benefit from it

15. To obtain good results from the use of role-play in training, a trainer should give participants

    A. a minimum of information about the situation so that they can act spontaneously
    B. scripts which illustrate the best method for handling the situation
    C. a complete explanation of the problem and the roles to be acted out
    D. a summary of work problems which involve interpersonal relations

Questions 16-20.

DIRECTIONS: Questions 16 through 20 are to be answered SOLELY on the basis of the following passage.

The dynamics of group behavior may be summed up by saying that the individuals in a group respond to many lines of force arising out of their relationship with every other member of a group and with the group itself. In addition, each member of a group quite naturally brings with him all the things that have been *bugging* him. Then, the situation or the setting in which the group meets, as well as the circumstances related to the formation of the group, are active working forces exerting some X influence upon each member of the group. Lastly, all of this kinetic energy is at the control of the person seeking to lead the group into some kind of action. If he is to produce something meaningful with the members of a group, he must utilize this energy, contain it, dissipate it in some fashion, or be faced with difficulty.

This dynamic force inherent in any group can be harnessed by a supervisor with leadership qualities, but it must be controlled. It will not be contained by acting without consultation with group members, by refusing to accept suggestions coming from the group, or by refusing to explain or even give notice of contemplated actions. However, it can be controlled by placing the focus upon the members of the group, rather than upon the supervisor, and depending upon the leader-supervisor to provide as many participative experiences for group members as is commensurate with his own decision-making responsibilities. It is true that this is subordinate-centered leadership, but the supervisor can gain strength through permissive leadership without sacrificing basic responsibilities for effective planning and adequate control of operations.

16. Of the following titles, the one that MOST closely describes the reading selection is

    A. THE SUPERVISOR WITH DYNAMIC LEADERSHIP POTENTIAL
    B. DISSIPATION OF GROUP ENERGY
    C. CONTROLLING GROUP RELATIONSHIPS
    D. SACRIFICING BASIC RESPONSIBILITIES

17. According to the above passage, the setting in which the group meets

    A. can readily be modified either in whole or in part
    B. must be made meaningful in some fashion to foster skills development
    C. can provide the sole source of group dynamics
    D. is one of the forces exerting influence on group members

18. According to the above passage, the members of the group

    A. should control their formation and development
    B. should control the circumstances of their meeting
    C. are influenced by the forces creating the group
    D. dissipate meaningless energy

19. According to the above passage, the effective group leader

    A. controls the focus of the group
    B. focuses his control over the group
    C. controls group forces by focusing upon group members
    D. focuses the group's forces upon himself

20. According to the above passage, effective leadership consists in
    A. partially compromising decision-making responsibilities
    B. partially sacrificing some basic responsibilities
    C. sometimes cultivating permissive subordinates
    D. providing participation for members of the group consistent with decision-making imperatives

20.___

Questions 21-22.

DIRECTIONS: Questions 21 and 22 are to be answered SOLELY on the basis of the following passage.

This country was built on the puritanical belief that honest toil was the foundation of moral rectitude, the cement of society, and the uphill road to progress. Idleness was sin. As a result, we treat free time today as a conditional joy. We permit outselves to relax only as a reward for hard work or as the recreation needed to put us back into shape for the job. Thus, the aimless delightful play of children gives way in adult life to a serious dedication to golf, the game that is so good for business.

21. According to the above passage, during former times in this country respectable work was considered to be MOST NEARLY a
    A. way to improve health
    B. form of recreation
    C. developer of good character
    D. reward for leisure

21.___

22. According to the point of view presented in the above passage, it would be MOST reasonable to assume that an employer would consider an employee's vacation to be a time for the employee to
    A. determine his own leisure time priorities
    B. loaf and relax
    C. learn new recreational skills
    D. increase his effectiveness at work

22.___

Questions 23-24.

DIRECTIONS: Questions 23 and 24 are to be answered SOLELY on the basis of the following passage.

A recent study revealed some very concrete evidence concerning the relationship between avocations and mental health. A number of well-adjusted persons were surveyed as to the type, number, and duration of their hobbies. The findings were compared to those from a similar survey of mentally disturbed persons. In the well-adjusted group, both the number of hobbies and the intensity with which they were pursued were far greater than that of the mentally disturbed group.

23. According to the above passage, the study showed that

    A. well-adjusted people engage in hobbies more widely and deeply than do mentally disturbed people
    B. hobbies, if taken seriously, serve to keep most people mentally well
    C. mental patients should be taught hobbies as a part of their therapy
    D. the degree of interest in hobbies plays an important role in maintaining good mental health

24. In reference to the study mentioned in the above passage, it is MOST accurate to say that it appears to have

    A. been based on a carefully-structured, complex research design
    B. considered the variables of mental health and hobby involvement
    C. contained a general definition of mental health
    D. given evidence of a causal relationship between hobbies and mental health

25. Across the years, our social sense has decreed that every position of social leadership, every place of influence, every concentration of social power in the hands of an individual, every instrument or agency that has aggregated to itself the power to affect the common welfare, has become by that very fact a social trust that must be administered for the common good. In our moral world, the social obligations of power are real and unescapable. On the basis of this statement, it would be MOST correct to state that

    A. an individual engaged in private enterprise does not have the social responsibility of one who holds public office
    B. social leadership carries with it the obligation to administer for the public good
    C. in our moral world, the abuse of the power is real and unescapable
    D. social leadership depends upon the aggregation of power in the hands of an individual or in an agency that wields concentrated influence

KEY (CORRECT ANSWERS)

1. B
2. C
3. A
4. C
5. C

6. A
7. A
8. A
9. C
10. C

11. D
12. C
13. A
14. A
15. C

16. C
17. D
18. C
19. C
20. D

21. C
22. D
23. A
24. B
25. B

TEST 2

DIRECTIONS: Each question or incomplete statement is followed by several suggested answers or completions. Select the one that BEST answers the question or completes the statement. *PRINT THE LETTER OF THE CORRECT ANSWER IN THE SPACE AT THE RIGHT.*

Questions 1-9.

DIRECTIONS: Questions 1 through 9 are to be answered SOLELY on the basis of the following passage.

The establishment of a procedure whereby the client's rent is paid directly by the Social Service agency has been suggested recently by many people in the Social Service field. It is believed that such a procedure would be advantageous to both the agency and the client. Under the current system, clients often complain that their rent allowances are not for the correct amount. Agencies, in turn, have had to cope with irate landlords who complain that they are not receiving rent checks until much later than their due date.

The proposed new system would involve direct payment of the client's rent by the agency to the landlord. Clients would not receive a monthly rent allowance. Under one possible implementation of such a system, special rent payment offices would be set up in each borough and staffed by Social Service clerical personnel. Each office would handle all work involved in sending out monthly rent payments. Each client would receive monthly notification from the Social Service agency that his rent has been paid. A rent office would be established for every three Social Service centers in each borough. Only in cases where the rental exceeds $350 per month would payment be made and records kept by the Social Service center itself rather than a special rent office. However, clients would continue to make all direct contacts through the Social Service center.

Files in the rent offices would be organized on the basis of client rental. All cases involving monthly rents up to, but not exceeding, $300 would be placed in salmon-colored folders. Cases with rents from $300 to $500 would be placed in buff folders, and those with rents exceeding $500, but less than $750 would be filed in blue folders. If a client's rental changed, he would be required to notify the center as soon as possible so that this information could be brought up-to-date in his folder and the color of his folder changed if necessary. Included in the information needed, in addition to the amount of rent, are the size of the apartment, the type of heat, and the number of flights of stairs to climb if there is no elevator.

Discussion as to whether the same information should be required of clients residing in city projects was resolved with the decision that the identical system of filing and updating of files should apply to such project tenants. The basic problem that might arise from the institution of such a program is that clients would resent being unable to pay their own rent. However, it is likely that such resentment would be only a temporary reaction to change and would disappear after the new system became standard procedure. It has been suggested that this program first be experimented with on a small scale to determine what problems may arise and how the program can be best implemented.

1. According to the above passage, there a number of complaints about the current system of rent payments. Which of the following is a complaint expressed in the passage?   1.____

A. Landlords complain that clients sometimes pay the wrong amount for their rent.
B. Landlords complain that clients sometimes do not pay their rent on time.
C. Clients say that the Social Service agency sometimes does not mail the rent out on time.
D. Landlords say that they sometimes fail to receive a check for the rent.

2. Assume that there are 15 Social Service centers in Manhattan.
   According to the above passage, the number of rent offices that should be established in that borough under the new system is

   A. 1   B. 3   C. 5   D. 15

3. According to the above passage, a client under the new system would receive

   A. a rent receipt from the landlord indicating that Social Services has paid the rent
   B. nothing since his rent has been paid by Social Services
   C. verification from the landlord that the rent was paid
   D. notices of rent payment from the Social Service agency

4. According to the above passage, a case record involving a client whose rent has changed from $310 to $540 per month should be changed from a _____ folder to a _____ folder.

   A. blue; salmon-colored   B. buff; blue
   C. salmon-colored; blue   D. yellow; buff

5. According to the above passage, if a client's rental is lowered because of violations in his building, he would be required to notify the

   A. building department   B. landlord
   C. rent payment office   D. Social Service center

6. Which one of the following kinds of information about a rented apartment is NOT mentioned in the above passage as being necessary to include in the client's folder?
   The

   A. floor number, if in an apartment house with an elevator
   B. rental, if in a city project apartment
   C. size of the apartment, if in a two-family house
   D. type of heat, if in a city project apartment

7. Assume that the rent payment proposal discussed in the above passage is approved and ready for implementation in the city.
   Which of the following actions is MOST in accordance with the proposal described in the above passage?

   A. Change over completely and quickly to the new system to avoid the confusion of having clients under both systems.
   B. Establish rent payment offices in all of the existing Social Service centers.
   C. Establish one small rent payment office in Manhattan for about six months.
   D. Set up an office in each borough and discontinue issuing rent allowances.

8. According to the above passage, it can be inferred that the MOST important drawback of the new system would be that once a program is started clients might feel

A. they have less independence than they had before
B. unable to cope with problems that mature people should be able to handle
C. too far removed from Social Service personnel to successfully adapt to the new requirements
D. too independent to work with the system

9. The above passage suggests that the proposed rent program be started as a pilot program rather than be instituted immediately throughout the city.
Of the following possible reasons for a pilot program, the one which is stated in the above passage as the MOST direct reason is that

   A. any change made would then be only on a temporary basis
   B. difficulties should be determined from small-scale implementation
   C. implementation on a wide scale is extremely difficult
   D. many clients might resent the new system

Questions 10-14.

DIRECTIONS: Questions 10 through 14 are to be answered SOLELY on the basis of the following passage.

PROCEDURE TO OBTAIN REIMBURSEMENT FROM DEPARTMENT OF HEALTH FOR CARE OF PHYSICALLY HANDICAPPED CHILDREN

Application for reimbursement must be received by the Department of Health within 30 days of the date of hospital admission in order that the Department of Hospitals may be reimbursed from the date of admission. Upon determination that patient is physically handicapped, as defined under Chapter 780 of the State Laws, the ward clerk shall prepare seven copies of Department of Health Form A-1 or A-2, Application and Authorization, and shall submit six copies to the institutional Collections Unit. The ward clerk shall also initiate two copies of Department of Health Form B-1 or B-2, Financial and Social Report, and shall forward them to the institutional Collections Unit for completion of Page 1 and routing to the Social Service Division for completion of the Social Summary on Page 2. Social Service Division shall return Form B-1 or B-2 to the institutional Collections Unit which shall forward one copy of Form B-1 or B-2 and six copies of Form A-1 or A-2 to Central Office Division of Collections for transmission to Bureau of Handicapped Children, Department of Health.

10. According to the above paragraph, the Department of Health will pay for hospital care for

    A. children who are physically handicapped
    B. any children who are ward patients
    C. physically handicapped adults and children
    D. thirty days for eligible children

11. According to the procedure described in the above paragraph, the definition of what constitutes a physical handicap is made by the

    A. attending physician
    B. laws of the State
    C. Social Service Division
    D. ward clerk

12. According to the above paragraph, Form B-1 or B-2 is   12.___
    A. a three page form containing detachable pages
    B. an authorization form issued by the Department of Hospitals
    C. completed by the ward clerk after the Social Summary has been entered
    D. sent to the institutional Collections Unit by the Social Service Division

13. According to the above paragraph, after their return by the Social Service Division, the   13.___
    institutional Collections Unit keeps

    A. one copy of Form A-1 or A-2
    B. one copy of Form A-1 or A-2 and one copy of Form B-1 or B-2
    C. one copy of Form B-1 or B-2
    D. no copies of Forms A-1 or A-2 or B-1 or B-2

14. According to the above paragraph, forwarding the *Application and Authorization* to the   14.___
    Department of Health is the responsibility of the

    A. Bureau for Handicapped Children
    B. Central Office Division of Collections
    C. Institutional Collections Unit
    D. Social Service Division

Questions 15-19.

DIRECTIONS: Questions 15 through 19 are to be answered SOLELY on the basis of the following *total annual income adjustment* rules for household income.

The basic annual income is to be calculated by multiplying the total of the current weekly salaries of all adults (age 21 or over) by 52.

Upward and downward adjustments must be made to the basic annual salary to arrive at the *total adjusted annual income* for the household.

UPWARD ADJUSTMENTS

1. Add one-half of total overtime payments in the previous two years.
2. Add that part of the earnings of any minor in the household that exceeded $3,000 in the previous 12 months.

DOWNWARD ADJUSTMENTS

1. Deduct one-third of all educational tuition payments for household members in the previous 12 months.
2. Deduct the expense of going to and from work in excess of $30 per week per household member. This adjustment is made on the basis of the previous 12 months and should be computed for each household member individually for each week in which excess travel expenses were incurred.
3. Deduct that part of child care expenses which exceeded $1,500 in the previous 12 months.

15. In Household A, the husband has a weekly salary of $585 and the wife has just had her salary increased from $390 to $420 per week. In the previous 12 months, each had a paid continuous vacation of four weeks; the husband had to travel to a secondary work location every fourth week. His travel costs during those weeks were $42 per week. In the previous 12 months, they had child care costs of $1,470.
What is the TOTAL annual adjusted income for the household?

    A. $52,116   B. $52,104   C. $51,828   D. $51,234

15.____

16. In Household B, the husband has a weekly salary of $540. In the past year, he received overtime payments of $255. In the year before that, he received overtime payments of $1,221. His wife has just begun a job with a weekly salary of $330. As a result of this, annual child care expenses will be $2,130.
What is the TOTAL annual adjusted income for the household?

    A. $45,240   B. $45,348   C. $45,978   D. $46,824

16.____

17. In Household C, the husband has a weekly salary of $555. The wife has a weekly salary of $390. They each had expenses of $33 per week when traveling to and from work in the previous 12 months. The husband had an annual paid vacation of five weeks, and the wife had an annual paid vacation of three weeks in the previous year. There is a daughter in college for whom annual tuition payments of $1,710 were made in the previous 12 months.
What is the TOTAL annual adjusted income for the household?

    A. $48,258   B. $48,282   C. $49,140   D. $50,022

17.____

18. In Household D, the husband has a weekly salary of $465, the wife has a weekly salary of $330, and an adult daughter has a weekly salary of $285. The husband received overtime payments of $1,890 in the past year. In the year before that, he received no overtime payments. In the past year, there were weekly child care expenses of $210 per week for 47 weeks.
What is the TOTAL adjusted annual income for the household?

    A. $57,105   B. $48,735   C. $47,235   D. $46,845

18.____

19. In Household E, the husband has a weekly salary of $615. The wife has a weekly salary of $195. During the past year, there were tuition payments of $255 per month for 10 months per year for children in grade school and annual tuition payments of $2,310 for a boy in high school. What is the TOTAL adjusted annual income for the household?

    A. $39,570   B. $39,690   C. $40,500   D. $42,120

19.____

Questions 20-22.

DIRECTIONS: Questions 20 through 22 are to be answered SOLELY on the basis of the following paragraph.

    Effective December 1, 2004, tenants thereafter admitted to public housing projects shall pay rents in accordance with Schedule DV if they are veterans of the Gulf War, and in accordance with Schedule D if they are not Gulf War veterans. However, all recipients of public assistance shall pay rents in accordance with Schedule DW. Tenants of public housing projects prior to the effective date of this change will continue to pay rent in accordance with Schedule C2 if they are veterans of the Iraqi War or the Gulf War, in accordance with

Schedule C if they are not such veterans, and in accordance with Schedule CW if they receive public assistance and if they are not eligible to use the C2 Schedule. In addition, effective December 1, 2004, when a tenant is accepted for assistance by the Department of Welfare, if such acceptance requires that the tenant pay a new rental as outlined above, the effective date of the new rental is to be the first of the month following the date that the tenant is accepted for assistance by the Department of Welfare instead of the first of the month following the date of application for public assistance.

20. John Jones, a Gulf War veteran, has been living in a public housing project since June 2003. He applied for public assistance on November 15, 2004 and was accepted for public assistance on December 17, 2004.
    If he continues to receive public assistance, his present rent should be based on the _____ Schedule.

    A. C2 B. CW C. DV D. DW

21. Jack Smith, who is not a veteran, moves into a public housing project in January 2006. If it should become necessary for him to apply for public assistance on February 10, 2006 and should he be accepted for such assistance on March 5, 2006, the rent that he pays in March 2006 should be based on the _____ Schedule.

    A. C B. CW C. D D. DW

22. John Doe, a veteran of the Iraqi War, was admitted to a public housing project in August 2004. He applied for public assistance on February 1, 2005 and was accepted for such assistance on March 1, 2005.
    On April 1, 2005, his rent should

    A. change to the C2 Schedule
    B. remain on the C2 Schedule, as previously
    C. change to the CW Schedule
    D. remain on the CW Schedule, as previously

Questions 23-25.

DIRECTIONS: Questions 23 through 25 are to be answered SOLELY on the basis of the following paragraph.

It has been proposed that an act be passed to provide for family allowances in the form of cash payments, normally to mothers, for children under sixteen years of age. Allowances are supposed to be spent exclusively for the care and education of the children; otherwise, they may be discontinued. They would vary in amount according to the age of the child and would be conditional upon satisfactory school attendance and accomplishment. The allowance would be paid to all families, regardless of means, but income tax exemptions for dependents would be reduced in consequence. The act would also permit the withdrawal of children from school and their entrance into the labor market after completing eighth grade. However, there would be no financial advantage in sending a child to work since the allowances would approximate the child's net earnings. Proponents of this proposal claim as advantages that it would provide social justice by taking into account elements of family need not possible under any normal wage structure system, be simple to administer, encourage an increase in the birth rate, remove unwilling or incapable students from our middle schools, and provide financial aid to poor, large families without the stigma of public welfare.

23. According to the proposal, the one of the following factors which would be LEAST likely to cause a variation in the amount of the allowance to a family or cause a discontinuance of it is

    A. a change in family wealth
    B. poor school attendance record of a child
    C. a child's being left back
    D. use of the allowance money on a hobby of one of the parents

23.____

24. The LEAST accurate of the following statements concerning schooling under this proposal is:

    A. A 14-year-old girl attending the 6th grade of elementary school will not be permitted to leave school, even though her school work is unsatisfactory.
    B. A poor family will be encouraged to continue the schooling of their 15-year-old twins who are in the junior year of high school.
    C. A 14-year-old boy who has been graduated from elementary school, but whose school attendance has been unsatisfactory, will not be permitted to attend high school.
    D. The family of a 17-year-old high school senior who is an honor student will not receive an allowance.

24.____

25. College attendance of bright children of poor families may be aided by this proposal because

    A. such children will be assured of higher marks
    B. families are likely to be smaller and consequently parents will be better able to send their children to college
    C. more scholarships are likely to be offered by private colleges as a result of this proposal
    D. the financial subsidy granted for a child under 16 may help the family save money towards a college education

25.____

KEY (CORRECT ANSWERS)

1.	B	11.	B
2.	C	12.	D
3.	D	13.	C
4.	B	14.	B
5.	D	15.	A
6.	A	16.	C
7.	C	17.	B
8.	A	18.	B
9.	B	19.	C
10.	A	20.	A

21. C
22. B
23. A
24. C
25. D

———

PREPARING WRITTEN MATERIAL
EXAMINATION SECTION
TEST 1

DIRECTIONS: Each of the following sentences may be classified under one of the following four categories:
A. *Faulty* because of incorrect grammar or usage
B. *Faulty* because of incorrect punctuation or spelling
C. *Faulty* because of incorrect capitalization
D. *Correct*

Examine each sentence carefully. Then, in the correspondingly numbered space on the right, print the capital letter preceding the option which is the best of the four suggested above.

(All incorrect sentences contain but one type of error. Consider a sentence correct if it contains none of the types of errors mentioned, even though there may be other correct ways of expressing the same thought.

1. They gave the poor man some food when he approached. 1.____
2. I regret the loss caused by the error. 2.____
3. The students have a new teacher for shop mantenance. 3.____
4. They sweared to bring out all the facts. 4.____
5. He decided to open a branch store on 33rd street. 5.____
6. His speed is equal and more than that of a racehorse. 6.____
7. He felt very warm on that Summer day. 7.____
8. He was assisted by his friend, who lives in the next house. 8.____
9. The climate of New York is colder than California. 9.____
10. I shall wait for you on the corner. 10.____
11. Did we see the boy whose the leader? 11.____
12. Being a modest person, John seldom takes about his invention. 12.____
13. The gang is called the smith street boys. 13.____
14. He seen the man break into the store. 14.____

145

15. We expected to lay still there for quite a while.
16. He is considered to be the Leader of his organization.
17. Although He received an invitation, He won't go.
18. The letter must be here some place.
19. I thought it to be he.
20. We expect to remain here for a long time.
21. The committee was agreed.
22. Two-thirds of the building are finished.
23. The water was froze.
24. Everyone of the salesmen must supply their own car.
25. Who is the author of Gone With the Wind?
26. He marched on and declaring that he would never surrender.
27. Who shall I say called?
28. Everyone has left but they.
29. Who did we give the order to?
30. Send your order in immediately.
31. I believe I paid the Bill.
32. I have not met but one person.
33. Why aren't Tom, and Fred, going to the dance?
34. What reason is there for him not going?
35. The seige of Malta was a tremendous event.
36. I was there yesterday I assure you.
37. Your ukulele is better than mine.
38. No one was there only Mary.

39. The Capital city of Vermont is Montpelier. 39.____

40. Reggie Jackson may hit the largest amount of home runs this season. 40.____

KEY (CORRECT ANSWERS)

1.	B	11.	B	21.	D	31.	C
2.	D	12.	D	22.	A	32.	A
3.	B	13.	C	23.	A	33.	B
4.	A	14.	A	24.	A	34.	A
5.	C	15.	A	25.	B	35.	B
6.	A	16.	C	26.	A	36.	B
7.	C	17.	C	27.	D	37.	B
8.	D	18.	A	28.	D	38.	A
9.	A	19.	A	29.	A	39.	C
10.	D	20.	D	30.	D	40.	A

TEST 2

Questions 1-3.

DIRECTIONS: Questions 1 through 3 each consist of four sentences. Choose the one sentence in each set of four that would be BEST for a formal letter or report. Consider grammar and appropriate usage.

1. A. Most all the work he completed before he become ill.
   B. He completed most of the work before becoming ill.
   C. Prior to him becoming ill his work was mostly completed.
   D. Before he became will most of the work he had completed.

2. A. Being that the report lacked a clearly worded recommendation, it did not matter that it contained enough information.
   B. There was enough information in the report, although it, including the recommendation, were not clearly worded.
   C. Although the report contained enough information, it did not have a clearly worded recommendation.
   D. Though the report did not have a recommendation that was clearly worded, and the information therein contained was enough.

3. A. Having already overlooked the important mistakes, the ones which she found were not as important toward the end of the letter.
   B. Toward the end of the letter she had already overlooked the important mistakes, so that which she had found were not important.
   C. The mistakes which she had already overlooked were not as important as those which near the end of letter she had found.
   D. The mistakes which she found near the end of the letter were not so important as those which she had already overlooked.

Questions 4-5.

DIRECTIONS: Select the correct answer.

4. The unit has exceeded _____ goals and the employees are satisfied with _____ accomplishments.
   A. their; it's   B. it's, it's   C. is, there   D. its, their

5. Research indicates that employees who _____ no opportunity for close social relationships often find their work unsatisfying, and this _____ of satisfaction often reflects itself in low production.
   A. have, lack   B. have, excess   C. has, lack   D. has, excess

KEY (CORRECT ANSWERS)

1. B
2. C
3. D
4. D
5. A

TEST 3

DIRECTIONS: Select the choice which BEST expresses the thought and which contains NO errors in grammar or sentence construction.

1. A. She, hearing a signal, the source lamp flashed.
   B. While hearing a signal, the source lamp flashed
   C. In hearing a signal, the source lamp flashed.
   D. As she heard a signal, the source lamp flashed.

   1.____

2. A. Every one of the time records have been initialed in the designated spaces.
   B. All of the time records has been initialed in the designated spaces.
   C. Which one of the time records was initialed in the designated spaces.
   D. The time records all been initialed in the designated spaces.

   2.____

3. A. If there is no one else to answer the phone, you will have to answer it.
   B. You will have to answer it yourself if no one else answers the phone.
   C. If no one else is not around to pick up the phone, you have to do it.
   D. You will have to answer the phone when nobodys here to do it.

   3.____

4. A. Dr. Byrnes not in his office. What could I do for you?
   B. Dr. Byrnes is not in his office. Is there something I can do for you?
   C. Since Dr. Byrnes is not in his office, might there be something I may do for you?
   D. Is there any ways I can assist you since Dr. Brynes is not in his office?

   4.____

5. A. She do not understand how the new console works.
   B. The way the new console works, she doesn't understand.
   C. She doesn't understand how the new console works.
   D. The new console works, so that she doesn't understand.

   5.____

KEY (CORRECT ANSWERS)

1. D
2. C
3. A
4. B
5. C

TEST 4

DIRECTIONS: The following questions each consist of a sentence which may or may not be an example of good English usage.

Consider grammar, punctuation, spelling, capitalization, awkwardness, etc.

Examine each sentence and then choose the correct statement about it from the four choices below. If the English usage in the sentence given is better than any of the changes suggested in options B, C, or D, choose option A. (Do not choose an option that will change the meaning of the sentence.)

1. The typist used an extention cord in order to connect her typewriter to the outlet nearest to her desk.
   A. This is an example of acceptable writing.
   B. A period should be placed after the word "cord" and the word "in" should have a capital "I."
   C. A comma should be placed after the word "typewriter."
   D. The word "extention" should be spelled "extension."

   1.____

2. He would have went to the conference if he had received an invitation.
   A. This is an example of acceptable writing.
   B. The word "went" should be replaced by the word "gone."
   C. The word "had" should be replaced by "would have."
   D. The word "conference" should be spelled "conference."

   2.____

3. In order to make the report neater, he spent many hours rewriting it.
   A. This is an example of acceptable writing.
   B. The word "more" should be inserted before the word "neater."
   C. There should be a colon after the word "neater."
   D. The word "spent" should be changed to "have spent."

   3.____

4. His supervisor told him that he should of read the memorandum more carefully.
   A. This is an example of acceptable writing.
   B. The word "memorandum" should be spelled "memorandom."
   C. The word "of" should be replaced by the word "have."
   D. The word "carefully" should be replaced by the word "have."

   4.____

5. It was decided that two separate reports should be written.
   A. This is an example of acceptable writing.
   B. A comma should be inserted after the word "decided."
   C. The word "be" should be replaced by the word "been."
   D. A colon should be inserted after the word "that."

   5.____

6. She don't seem to understand that the work must be done as soon as possible.
   A. This is an example of acceptable writing.
   B. The word "doesn't" should replace the word "don't."
   C. The word "why" should replace the word "that."
   D. The word "as" before the word "soon" should be eliminated.

   6.____

KEY (CORRECT ANSWERS)

1. D
2. B
3. A
4. C
5. A
6. B

PREPARING WRITTEN MATERIAL

PARAGRAPH REARRANGEMENT
COMMENTARY

The sentences that follow are in scrambled order. You are to rearrange them in proper order and indicate the letter choice containing the correct answer at the space at the right.

Each group of sentences in this section is actually a paragraph presented in scrambled order. Each sentence in the group has a place in that paragraph; no sentence is to be left out. You are to read each group of sentences and decide upon the best order in which to put the sentences so as to form a well-organized paragraph.

The questions in this section measure the ability to solve a problem when all the facts relevant to its solution are not given.

More specifically, certain positions of responsibility and authority require the employee to discover connection between events sometimes, apparently, unrelated. In order to do this, the employee will find it necessary to correctly infer that unspecified events have probably occurred or are likely to occur. This ability becomes especially important when action must be taken on incomplete information.

Accordingly, these questions require competitors to choose among several suggested alternatives, each of which presents a different sequential arrangement of the events. Competitors must choose the MOST logical of the suggested sequences.

In order to do so, they may be required to draw on general knowledge to infer missing concepts or events that are essential to sequencing the given events. Competitors should be careful to infer only what is essential to the sequence. The plausibility of the wrong alternatives will always require the inclusion of unlikely events or of additional chains of events which are NOT essential to sequencing the given events.

It's very important to remember that you are looking for the best of the four possible choices, and that the best choice of all may not even be one of the answers you're given to choose from.

There is no one right way to solve these problems. Many people have found it helpful to first write out the order of the sentences, as they would have arranged them, on their scrap paper before looking at the possible answers. If their optimum answer is there, this can save them some time. If it isn't, this method can still give insight into solving the problem. Others find it most helpful to just go through each of the possible choices, contrasting each as they go along. You should use whatever method feels comfortable and works for you.

While most of these types of questions are not that difficult, we've added a higher percentage of the difficult type, just to give you more practice. Usually there are only one or two questions on this section that contain such subtle distinctions that you're unable to answer confidently. And you then may find yourself stuck deciding between two possible choices, neither of which you're sure about.

PREPARING WRITTEN MATERIAL
PARAGRAPH REARRANGEMENT
EXAMINATION SECTION
TEST 1

DIRECTIONS: The following groups of sentences need to be arranged in an order that makes sense. Select the letter preceding the sequence that represents the best sentence order. *PRINT THE LETTER OF THE CORRECT ANSWER IN THE SPACE AT THE RIGHT.*

1. I. The ostrich egg shell's legendary toughness makes it an excellent substitute for certain types of dishes or dinnerware, and in parts of Africa ostrich shells are cut and decorated for use as containers for water.
    II. Since prehistoric times, people have used the enormous egg of the ostrich as a part of their diet, a practice which has required much patience and hard work—to hard boil an ostrich egg takes about four hours.
    III. Opening the egg's shell, which is rock hard and nearly an inch thick, requires heavy tools, such as a saw or chisel; from inside, a baby ostrich must use a hornlike projection on its beak as a miniature pick-axe to escape from the egg.
    IV. The offspring of all higher-order animals originate from single egg cells that are carried by mothers, and most of these eggs are relatively small, often microscopic.
    V. The egg of the African ostrich, however, weighs a massive thirty pounds, making it the largest single cell on earth, and a common object of human curiosity and wonder.
    The BEST order is:
    A. V, IV, I, II, III   B. I, IV, V, III, II   C. IV, II, III, V, I   D. IV, V, II, III, I

1.____

2. I. Typically only a few feet high on the open sea, individual tsunami have been known to circle the entire globe two or three times if their progress is not interrupted, but are not usually dangerous until they approach the shallow water that surrounds land masses.
    II. Some of the most terrifying and damaging hazards caused by earthquakes are tsunami, which were once called "tidal waves"—a poorly chosen name, since these waves have nothing to do with tides.
    III. Then a wave, slowed by the sudden drag on the lower part of its moving water column, will pile upon itself, sometimes reaching a height of over 100 feet.
    IV. Tsunami (Japanese for "great harbor wave") are seismic waves that are caused by earthquakes near oceanic trenches, and once triggered, can travel up to 600 miles an hour on the open ocean.
    V. A land-shoaling tsunami is capable of extraordinary destruction; some tsunami have deposited large boats miles inland, washed out two-foot-thick seawalls, and scattered locomotive trains over long distances.
    The BEST order is:
    A. IV, I, III, II, V   B. I, III, IV, II, V   C. V, I, III, II, IV   D. II, IV, I, III, V

2.____

155

3. I. Soon, by the 1940s, jazz was the most popular type of music among American intellectuals and college students.
    II. In the early days of jazz, it was considered "lowdown" music, or music that was played only in rough, disreputable bars and taverns.
    III. However, jazz didn't take too long to develop from early ragtime melodies into more complex, sophisticated forms, such as Charlie Parker's "bebop" style of jazz.
    IV. After charismatic band leaders such as Duke Ellington and Count Basie brought jazz to a larger audience, and jazz continued to evolve into more complicated forms, white audiences began to accept and even to enjoy the new American art form.
    V. Many white Americans, who then dictated the tastes of society, were wary of music that was played almost exclusively in black clubs in the poorer sections of cities and towns.
    The BEST order is:
    A. V, IV, III, II, I
    B. II, V, III, IV, I
    C. IV, V, III, I, II
    D. I, II, IV, III, V

3.____

4. I. Then, hanging in a windless place, the magnetized end of the needle would always point to the south.
    II. The needle could then be balanced on the rim of a cup, or the edge of a fingernail, but this balancing act was hard to maintain, and the needle often fell off.
    III. Other needles would point to the north, and it was important for any traveler finding his way with a compass to remember which kind of magnetized needle he was carrying.
    IV. To make some of the earliest compasses in recorded history, ancient Chinese "magicians" would rub a needle with a piece of magnetized iron called a lodestone.
    V. A more effective method of keeping the needle free to swing with its magnetic pull was to attach a strand of silk to the center of the needle with a tiny piece of wax.
    The BEST order is:
    A. IV, II, V, I, III
    B. IV, III, V, II, I
    C. IV, V, II, I, III
    D. IV, I, III, V, II

4.____

5. I The now-famous first mate of the *H.M.S. Bounty*, Fletcher Christian, founded one of the world's most peculiar civilizations in 1790.
    II. The men knew they had just committed a crime for which they could be hanged, so they set sail for Pitcairn, a remote, abandoned island in the far eastern region of the Polynesian archipelago, accompanied by twelve Polynesian women and six men.
    III. In a mutiny that has become legendary, Christian and the others forced Captain Bligh into a lifeboat and set him adrift off the coast of Tonga in April of 1789.
    IV. In early 1790, the *Bounty* landed at Pitcairn Island, where the men lived out the rest of their lives and founded an isolated community which to this day includes direct descendants of Christian and the other Crewmen.

5.____

V. The *Bounty*, commanded by Captain William Bligh, was in the middle of a global voyage, and Christian and his shipmates had come to the conclusion that Bligh was a reckless madman who would lead them to their deaths unless they took the ship from him.

The BEST order is:
A. IV, V, III, II, I   B. I, III, V, II, IV   C. I, V, III, II, IV   D. III, I, V, IV, II

6. I. But once the vines had been led to make orchids, the flowers had to be carefully hand-pollinated, because unpollinated orchids usually lasted less than a day, wilting and dropping off the vine before it had even become dark.
    II. The Totonac farmers discovered that looping a vine back around once it reached a five-foot height on its host tree would cause the vine to flower.
    III. Though they knew how to process the fruit pods and extract vanilla's flavoring agent, the Totonacs also knew that a wild vanilla vine did not produce abundant flowers or fruit.
    IV. Wild vines climbed along the trunks and canopies of trees, and this constant upward growth diverted most of the vine's energy to making leaves instead of the orchid flowers that once pollinated, would produce the flavorful pods.
    V. Hundreds of years before vanilla became a prized food flavoring in Europe and the Western World, the Totonac Indians of the Mexican Gulf Coast were skilled cultivators of the vanilla vine, whose fruit they literally worshipped as a goddess.

    The BEST order is:
    A. II, III, IV, I, V   B. II, IV, III, I, V   C. V, III, IV, II, I   D. III, IV, I, II, V

7. I. Once airborne, the spider is at the mercy of the air currents—usually the spider takes a brief journey, traveling close to the ground, but some have been found in air samples collected as high as 10,000 feet, or been reported landing on ships far out at sea.
    II. Once a young spider has hatched, it must leave the environment into which it was born as quickly as possible, in order to avoid competing with its hundreds of brothers and sisters for food.
    III. The silk rises into warm air currents, and as soon as the pull feels adequate the spider lets go and drifts up into the air, suspended from the silk strand in the same way that a person might parasail.
    IV. To help young spiders do this, many species have adapted a practice known as "aerial dispersal," or, in common speech, "ballooning."
    V. A spider that wants to leave its surroundings quickly will climb to the top of a grass system or twig, face into the wind, and aim its back end into the air, releasing a long stream of silk from the glands near the tip of its abdomen.

    The BEST order is:
    A. V, IV, II, III, I   B. V, II, IV, I, III   C. II, V, IV, III, I   D. II, IV, V, III, I

8. I. For about a year, Tycho worked at a castle in Prague with a scientist named Johannes Kepler, but their association was cut short by another argument that drove Kepler out of the castle, to later develop, on his own, the theory of planetary orbits.
    II. Tycho found life without a nose embarrassing, so he made a new nose for himself out of silver, which reportedly remained glued to his face for the rest of his life.
    III. Tycho Brahe, the 17th-century Danish astronomer, is today more famous for his odd and arrogant personality than for any contribution he has made to our knowledge of the stars and planets.
    IV. Early in his career, as a student at Rostock University, Tycho got into an argument with another student about who was the better mathematician, and the two became so angry that the argument turned into a sword fight, during which Tycho's nose was sliced off.
    V. Later in his life, Tycho's arrogance may have kept him from playing a part in one of the greatest astronomical discoveries in history: the elliptical orbits of the solar system's planets.
    The BEST order is:
    A. I, IV, II, III, V B. IV, II, III, V, I C. IV, II, I, III, V D. III, IV, II, V, I

9. I. The processionaries are so used to this routine that if a person picks up the end of a silk line and brings it back to the origin—creating a closed circle—the caterpillars may travel around and around for days, sometimes starving or freezing, without changing course.
    II. Rather than relying on sight or sound, the other caterpillars, who are lined up end-to-end behind the leader, travel to and from their nests by walking on this silk line, and each will reinforce it by laying down its own marking line as it passes over.
    III. In order to insure the safety of individuals, the processionary caterpillar nests in a tree with dozens of other caterpillars, and at night, when it is safest, they all leave together in search of food.
    IV. The processionary caterpillar of the European continent is a perfect illustration of how much some inspect species rely on instinct in their daily routines.
    V. As they leave their nests, the processionaries form a single-file line behind a leader who spins and lays out a silk line to mark the chosen path.
    The BEST order is:
    A. IV, III, V, II, I B. III, V, IV, II, I C. III, V, II, I, IV D. IV, V, III, I, II

10. I. Often, the child is also given a handcrafted walker or push cart, to provide support for its first upright explorations.
    II. In traditional Indian families, a child's first steps are celebrated as a ceremonial event, rooted in ancient myth.
    III. These carts are often intricately designed to resemble the chariot of Krishna, an important figure in Indian mythology.
    IV. The sound of these anklet bells is intended to mimic the footsteps of the legendary child Rama, who is celebrated in devotional songs throughout India.

V. When the child's parents see that the child is ready to begin walking, they will fit it with specially designed ankle bracelets, adorned with gently ringing bells.

The BEST order is:
A. II, III, IV, I, V B. II, V, III, I, IV C. V, IV, I, III, II D. V, III, II, I, IV

11.   I. The settlers planted Osage oranges all across Middle America, and today long lines and rectangles of Osage orange trees can still be seen on the prairies, running along the former boundaries of farms that no longer exist.
II. After trying sod walls and water-filled ditches with no success, American farmers began to look for a plant that was adaptable to prairie weather, and that could be trimmed into a hedge that was "pig-tight, horse-high, and bull-strong."
III. The tree, so named because it bore a large (but inedible) fruit the size of an orange, was among the sturdiest and hardiest of American trees, and was prized among Native Americans for the strength and flexibility of bows which were made from its wood.
IV. The first people to practice agriculture on the American flatlands were faced with an important problem: what would they use to fence their land in a place that was almost entirely without trees or rocks?
V. Finally, an Illinois farmer brought the settlers a tree that was native to the land between the Red and Arkansas rivers, a tree called the Osage orange.

The BEST order is:
A. II, I, V, III, IV B. I, II, III, IV, V C. IV, II, V, III, I D. IV, II, I, III, V

12.   I. After about ten minutes of such spirited and complicated activity, the head dancer is free to make up his or her own movements while maintaining the interest of the New Year's crowd.
II. The dancer will then perform a series of leg kicks, while at the same time operating the lion's mouth with his own hand and moving the ears and eyes by means of a string which is attached to the dancer's own mouth.
III. The most difficult role of this dance belongs to the one who controls the lion's head; this person must lead all the other "parts" of the lion through the choreographed segments of the dance.
IV. The head dancer begins with a complex series of steps. alternately stepping forward with the head raised, and then retreating a few steps while lowering the head, a movement that is intended to create the impression that the lion is keeping a watchful eye for anything evil.
V. When performing a traditional Chinese New Year's lion dance, several performers must fit themselves inside a large lion costume and work together to enact different parts of the dance.

The BEST order is:
A. V, III, IV, II, I B. III, IV, II, V, I C. III, I, V, IV, II D. IV, II, III, V, I

13. I. For many years the shell of the chambered nautilus was treasured in Europe for its beauty and intricacy, but collectors were unaware that they were in possession of the structure that marked a "missing link" in the evolution of marine mollusks.
    II. The nautilus, however, evolved a series of enclosed chambers in its shell, and invented a new use for the structure: the shell began to serve as a buoyancy device.
    III. Equipped with this new flotation device, the nautilus did not need the single, muscular foot of its predecessors, but instead developed flaps, tentacles, and a gentle form of jet propulsion that transformed it into the first mollusk able to take command of its own density and explore a three-dimensional world.
    IV. By pumping and adjusting air pressure into the chambers, the nautilus could spend the day resting on the bottom, and then rise toward the surface at night in search of food.
    V. The nautilus shell looks like a large snail shell, similar to those of its ancestors, who used their shells as protective coverings while they were anchored to the sea floor.

    The BEST order is:
    A. V, II, IV, I, III   B. V, I, II, III, IV   C. I, II, V, III, IV   D. I, V, II, IV, III

14. I. While France and England battled for control of the region, the Acadiens prospered on the fertile farmland, which was finally secured by England in 1713.
    II. Early in the 17th century, settlers from Western France founded a colony called Acadie in what is now the Canadian province of Nova Scotia.
    III. At this time, English officials feared the presence of spies among the Acadiens who might be loyal to their French homeland, and the Acadiens were deported to spots along the Atlantic and Caribbean shores of America.
    IV. The French settlers remained on this land, under English rule, for around forty years, until the beginning of the French and Indian War, another conflict between France and England.
    V. As the Acadien refugees drifted toward a final home in Southern Louisiana, neighbors shortened their name to "Cadien," and finally "Cajun," the name which the descendants of early Acadiens still call themselves.

    The BEST order is:
    A. I, IV, II, III, V   B. II, I, III, V, IV   C. II, I, IV, III, V   D. V, II, III, IV, I

15. I. Traditional households in the Eastern and Western regions of Africa serve two meals a day—one at around noon, and the other in the evening.
    II. The starch is then used in the way that Americans might use a spoon, to scoop up a portion of the main dish on the person's plate.
    III. The reason for the starch's inclusion in every meal has to do with taste as well as nutrition; African food can be very spicy, and the starch is known to cool the burning effect of the main dish.
    IV. When serving these meals, the main dish is usually served on individual plates, and the starch is served on a communal plate, from which diners break off a piece of bread or scoop rice or fufu in their fingers.

V. The typical meals usually consist of a thick stew or soup as the main course, and an accompanying starch—either bread, rice, or *fufu*, a starchy grain paste similar in consistency to mashed potatoes.

The BEST order is:

A. V, II, III, IV, I   B. V, I, IV, III, II   C. I, IV, V, III, II   D. I, V, IV, II, III

16.
- I. In the early days of the American Midwest, Indiana settlers sometimes came together to hold an event called an apple peeling, where neighboring settlers gathered at the homestead of a host family to help prepare the hosts' apple crop for cooking, canning, and making apple butter.
- II. At the beginning of the event, each peeler sat down in front of a ten- or twenty-gallon stone jar and was given a crock of apples and a paring knife.
- III. Once a peeler had finished with a crock, another was placed next to him; if the peeler was an unmarried man, he kept a strict count of the number of apples he had peeled, because the winner was allowed to kiss the girl of his choice.
- IV. The peeling usually ended by 9:30 in the evening, when the neighbors gathered in the host family's parlor for a dance social.
- V. The apples were peeled, cored, and quartered, and then placed into the jar.

The BEST order is:

A. I, V, III, IV, II   B. II, V, III, IV, I   C. I, II, V, III, IV   D. II, I, V, IV, III

17.
- I. If your pet turtle is a land turtle and is native to temperate climates, it will stop eating some time in October, which should be your cue to prepare the turtle for hibernation.
- II. The box should then be covered with a wire screen, which will protect the turtle from any rodents or predators that might want to take advantage of a motionless and helpless animal.
- III. When your turtle hasn't eaten for a while and appears ready to hibernate, it should be moved to its winter quarters, most likely a cellar or garage, where the temperature should range between 40° and 45°F.
- IV. Instead of feeding the turtle, you should bathe it every day in warm water, to encourage the turtle to empty its intestines in preparation for its long winter sleep.
- V. Here the turtle should be placed in a well-ventilated box whose bottom is covered with a moisture-absorbing layer of clay beads, and then filled three-fourths full with almost dry peat moss or wood chips, into which the turtle will burrow and sleep for several months.

The BEST order is:

A. I, IV, III, V, II   B. III, IV, II, V, I   C. III, II, IV, I, V   D. IV, V, II, III, I

18.
- I. Once he has reached the nest, the hunter uses two sturdy bamboo poles like huge chopsticks to pull the next away from the mountainside, into a large basket that will be lowered to people waiting below.
- II. The world's largest honeybees colonize the Nealese mountainsides, building honeycombs as large as a person on sheer rock faces that are often hundreds of feet high.

III. In the remote mountain country of Nepal, a small band of "honey hunters" carry out a tradition so ancient that 10,000 year-old drawings of the practice have been found in the caves of Nepal.
IV. To harvest the honey and beeswax from these combs, a honey hunter climbs above the nests, lowers a long bamboo-fiber ladder over the cliff, and then climbs down.
V. Throughout this dangerous practice, the hunter is stung repeatedly, and only the veterans, with skin that has been toughened over the years, are able to return from a hunt without the painful swelling caused by stings.

The BEST order is:
   A. II, IV, III, V, I   B. II, IV, I, V, III   C. V, III, II, IV, I   D. III, II, IV, I, V

19. I. After the Romans left Britain, there were relentless attacks on the islands from the barbarian tribes of northern Germany—the Angles, Saxons, and Jutes.
   II. As the empire weakened, Roman soldiers withdrew from Britain, leaving behind a country that continued to practice the Christian religion that had been introduced by the Romans.
   III. Early Latin writings tell of a Christian warrior named Arturius (Arthur, in English) who led the British citizens to defeat these barbarian invades, and brought an extended period of peace to the lands of Britain.
   IV. Long ago, the British Isles were part of the far-flung Roman Empire that extended across most of Europe and into Africa and Asia.
   V. The romantic legend of King Arthur and his knights of the Round Table, one of the most popular and widespread stories of all time, appears to have some foundation in history.

   The BEST order is:
      A. V, IV, III, II, I   B. V, IV, II, I, III   C. IV, V, II, III, I   D. IV, III, II, I, V

20. I. The cylinder was allowed to cool until it could stand on its own, and then it was cut from the tube and split down the side with a single straight cut.
   II. Nineteenth-century glassmakers, who had not yet discovered the glazier's modern techniques for making panes of glass, had to create a method for converting their blown gas into flat sheets.
   III. The bubble was then pierced at the end to make a hole that opened up while the glassmaker gently spun it, creating a cylinder of glass.
   IV. Turned on its side and laid on a conveyor belt, the cylinder was strengthened, or tempered, by being heated again and cooled very slowly, eventually flattening out into a single rectangular of glass.
   V. To do this, the glassmaker dipped the end of a long tube into melted glass and blew into the other end of the tube, creating an expanding bubble of glass.

   The BEST order is:
      A. II, V, III, IV, I   B. II, IV, V, III, I   C. III, V, II, IV, I   D. III, I, IV, V, II

21. I. The splints are almost always hidden, but horses are occasionally born whose splinted toes project from the leg on either side, just above the hoof.
    II. The second and fourth toes remained, but shrank to thin splints of bone that fused invisibly to the horse's leg bone.
    III. Horses are unique among mammals, having evolved feet that each end in what is essentially a single toe, capped by a large, sturdy hoof.
    IV. Julius Caesar, an emperor of ancient Rome, was said to have owned one of these three-toed horses, and considered it so special that he would not permit anyone else to ride it.
    V. Though the horse's earlier ancestors possessed the traditional mammalian set of five toes on each foot, the horse has retained only its third toe; its first and fifth toes disappeared completely as the horse evolved.
    The BEST order is:
    A. III, V, II, I, IV   B. V, III, II, IV, I   C. III, II, V, I, IV   D. V, II, III, I, IV

22. I. The new building materials—some of which are twenty feet long, and weigh nearly six tons—were transported to Pohnpei on rafts, and were brought into their present position by using hibiscus fiber ropes and leverage to move the stone columns upward along the inclined trunks of coconut palm trees.
    II. The ancestors built great fires to heat the stone, and then poured cool seawater on the columns, which caused the stone to contract and split along natural fracture lines.
    III. The now-abandoned enclave of Nan Madol, a group of 92 man-made islands off the shore of the Micronesian island of Pohnpei, is estimated to have been built around the year 500 A.D.
    IV. The islanders say their ancestors quarried stone columns from a nearby island, where large basalt columns were formed by the cooling of molten lava.
    V. The structures of Nan Madol are remarkable for the sheer size of some of the stone "longs" or columns that were used to create the walls of the offshore community, and today anthropologists can only rely on the information of existing local people for clues about how Nan Madol was built.
    The BEST order is:
    A. V, IV, III, II, I   B. V, III, I, IV, II   C. III, V, IV, II, I   D. III, I, IV, II, V

23. I. One of the most easily manipulated substances on earth, glass can be made into ceramic tiles that are composed of over 90% air.
    II. NASA's space shuttles are the first spacecraft ever designed to leave and re-enter the earth's atmosphere while remaining intact.
    III. These ceramic tiles are such effective insulators that when a tile emerges from the oven in which it was fired, it can be held safely in a person's hand by the edges while its interior still glows at a temperature well over 2000°F.
    IV. Eventually, the engineers were led to a material that is as old as our most ancient civilization.
    V. Because the temperature during atmospheric re-entry is so incredibly hot, it took NASA's engineers some time to find a substance capable of protecting the shuttles.

The BEST order is:
A. V, II, I, II, IV   B. II, V, IV, I, III   C. II, III, I, IV, V   D. V, IV, III, I, II

24. I. The secret to teaching any parakeet to talk is patience, and the understanding that when a bird talks," it is simply imitating what it hears, rather than putting ideas into words.
II. You should stay just out of sight of the bird and repeat the phrase you want it to learn, for at least fifteen minutes every morning and evening.
III. It is important to leave the bird without any words of encouragement or farewell; otherwise it might combine stray remarks or phrases, such as "Good night," with the phrase you are trying to teach it.
IV. For this reason, to train your bird to imitate your words you should keep it free of any distractions, especially other noises, while you are giving it "lesson."
V. After your repetition, you should quietly leave the bird alone for a while, to think over what it has just heard.
The BEST order is:
A. I, IV, II, V, III   B. I, II, IV, III, V   C. III, II, I, V, IV   D. III, I, V, IV, II

24.____

25. I. As a school approaches, fishermen from neighboring communities join their fishing boats together as a fleet, and string their gill nets together to make a huge fence that is held up by cork floats.
II. At a signal from the party leaders, or *nakura*, the family members pound the sides of the boats or beat the water with long poles, creating a sudden and deafening noise.
III. The fishermen work together to drag the trap into a half-circle that may reach 300 yards in diameter, and then the families move their boats to form the other half of the circle around the school of fish.
IV. The school of fish flee from the commotion into the awaiting trap, where a final wall of net is thrown over the open end of the half-circle, securing the day's haul.
V. Indonesian people from the area around the Sulu islands live on the sea, in floating villages made of lashed-together or stilted homes, and make much of their living by fishing their home waters for migrating schools of snapper, scad, and other fish.
The BEST order is:
A. I, V, III, IV, II   B. I, II, IV, III, V   C. V, I, II, III, IV   D. V, I, III, II, IV

25.____

KEY (CORRECT ANSWERS)

1.	D		11.	C
2.	D		12.	A
3.	B		13.	D
4.	A		14.	C
5.	C		15.	D
6.	C		16.	C
7.	D		17.	A
8.	D		18.	D
9.	A		19.	B
10.	B		20.	A

21. A
22. C
23. B
24. A
25. D

www.ingramcontent.com/pod-product-compliance
Lightning Source LLC
Chambersburg PA
CBHW080322020526
44117CB00035B/2603